Teaching the Primary Foundation Subjects

Teaching the Primary Foundation Subjects

Maggie Webster
Sarah Misra

McGraw Hill Education

Open University Press

Open University Press
McGraw-Hill Education
McGraw-Hill House
Shoppenhangers Road
Maidenhead
Berkshire
England
SL6 2QL

email: enquiries@openup.co.uk
world wide web: www.openup.co.uk

and Two Penn Plaza, New York, NY 10121-2289, USA

First published 2015

Copyright © Maggie Webster and Sarah Misra, 2015

A catalogue record of this book is available from the British Library

ISBN-13: 978-0-335-26376-9
ISBN-10: 0-335-26376-3
eISBN: 978-0-335-26377-6

Library of Congress Cataloging-in-Publication Data
CIP data applied for

Typeset by Aptara, Inc.
Printed and bound by CPI Group (UK) Ltd, Croydon, CR0 4YY

Praise for this book

"*An essential companion for both new and experienced educators of the Primary Curriculum. Webster and Misra draw on the pertinent knowledge and experience of subject specialists to deliver a modern, articulate and knowledgeable overview of how to effectively deliver the Foundation Subjects. Their passion for the Foundation Subjects is evident through their in-depth analysis of the value they have to the holistic development of children. Through a comprehensive examination of subject identity, effective pedagogy and creative teaching strategies, Webster and Misra provide the tools to be a pro-active, reflective and versatile leader in the Foundation Subjects. The knowledge and experience of the authors and contributors is evident in the book's ability to convey theory and pedagogy using coherent and accessible language, which makes it both informative and practical. This book adopts a unique and fresh approach which seamlessly combines theory and experience to deliver information that is enlightening, inspiring and truly useful.*"

Nick Murphy, Trainee teacher and Teaching Assistant, Edge Hill University, UK

"*This book fills a void in the world of ITE. The links between theory and practice can be difficult to comprehend for those making their first steps into the profession. With the three lens approach exploring the unique nature of each discipline synthesised with pedagogical aspects and creative ideas, this book provides fabulous support for trainee teachers to clearly make those links. I feel that 'Teaching the Primary Foundation Subjects' will be an invaluable text for ITE providers to share with their students to support and guide them not only through their placements but through their academic work too.*"

Emma McVittie, Senior Lecturer Primary and Secondary RE,
York St John University, UK

To our makers, keepers and angels
You know who you are

Contents

List of figures and tables

Figures

Tables

Notes on contributors

David Barker David is a senior lecturer in science education, although he has extensive experience of working with second language learners. Having studied modern languages for his first degree in the 1980s he was fortunate to be able to teach French throughout his career in both Key Stages 1 and 2 in a small primary school in Radcliffe near Manchester. He was part of the Pathfinder project for primary foreign languages from 2003 to 2005. David worked for two years (2005–2007) within ITE at Leeds Metropolitan University (now Leeds Beckett University), where he taught on the Primary French course; he was also involved in the rewriting of French CPD materials for the TDA during this time. From 2007 to 2014 David worked on the UG programme for ITE at Edge Hill University; he taught on the second year of the modern languages specialist option and feels passionate about the role that language learning has to play in the curriculum.

Wendy Dixon Wendy's teaching career has covered a number of roles. She has been school coordinator for design technology and an assessment coordinator. She has held positions of responsibility including educational visit coordinator, school staff mentor and Key Stage 2 leader, and was a member of the senior management team. She has delivered cluster insets and was cluster moderator of English writing.

Throughout her career Wendy has gained several professional achievements. She piloted ICT programmes and was teacher advocate for the Graduate Teaching Programme. As part of the trustee team representing the UK she also attended the International Charity conference in Belarus. Wendy has developed a number of areas of expertise, which reflect her varied professional practice; these include design technology, literacy, assessment and mixed-age teaching. She is the foundation subjects coordinator at Edge Hill University and also manages a large ICT project named Active Expression.

Mike Goulding Mike Goulding has been a member of the Primary and Early Years Team at Edge Hill University for more than seven years. He currently holds the position of subject leader for physical education. Throughout his career Mike has gained professional experience in a number of roles. In the primary school environment he was a class teacher as well as physical education coordinator. He was also an advisory teacher for physical education before becoming a senior lecturer and PE subject leader at Edge Hill University.

Mike has introduced Top Play and Top Sport training to schools in the Wirral followed by introducing schemes of Work for Physical Education for Wirral Education Authority. Recently he introduced the Start to Move programme in partnership with the Youth Sport Trust with his trainee teachers at Edge Hill University, which has been very successful in demonstrating how trainee teachers can have an impact on children's learning.

Marion Hobbs   Marion Hobbs has more than 25 years' experience in education. She has a number of qualifications, including BA (Hons) Geography from the University of Manchester, PGCE Primary Education from the University of Leeds and MA Educational Studies from Lancaster University. She has a particular professional interest in the impact of mentoring on the student experience and the development of the primary humanities curriculum with a focus on geography.

Marion has experience of being a member of the Geographical Association. Her involvement with that organisation has led to her attendance at geography teacher conferences and the annual Geographical Association conference. Marion's keen interest in her areas of academic expertise has led to her working with a local education Environmental Officer to develop an environmental bus to support the primary geography curriculum within the authority.

Sarah Misra   Sarah gained degrees in both history of art and design and business studies, and studied education in a museum setting at the V&A Museum in London, working in stage and costume design in the USA and as a children's books buyer before training as a teacher.

She has enjoyed a varied career in primary education having worked as a teacher across all primary year groups, teaching all subjects, and in a variety of different schools and areas. She has worked in the senior management team both in primary education and in higher education.

In 2011, she moved to Edge Hill University, where she worked as a senior lecturer in education and early years and led the Primary Foundation Subjects Team before moving to Staffordshire University as a senior lecturer and PGCE award leader. She has an MA in Education from Manchester Metropolitan Museum and is currently studying a Doctorate in Education at Chester University.

Chris Russell   As a primary classroom practitioner Chris gained considerable experience across both Key Stages. He held the roles of ICT coordinator, history coordinator, music coordinator, assessment coordinator, and gifted and talented coordinator. Shortly before joining Edge Hill University, Chris was also the cluster leader for modern foreign languages and worked with the National Trust at Speke Hall, Liverpool, and at Southport's Botanic Garden Museum.

At Edge Hill University, Chris is subject leader for primary history and is a member of the Primary and Early Years Computing Team. He is keen to make links between new technologies and the development of historical knowledge, skills and understanding. His interest in research has led to his input at the Primary History Conference in March 2012 and he has contributed to three issues of *Teach Primary*. He is a representative on the Faculty Research Committee and has been approached by a local primary school to help with the rewriting of its history schemes of work, emphasising an enquiry-based approach.

Ian Shirley   Ian Shirley has been a member of the Primary and Early Years Team for more than five years, and his qualification portfolio includes BEd (Hons) from King Alfred's College in Winchester and MA Psychology for Musicians from Sheffield University. He is also currently extending his reach by studying for an EdD at Sheffield University. Ian holds a number of roles at Edge Hill University and is the subject leader for primary music.

From 2003 to 2007 Ian was senior lecturer in primary music education at Canterbury Christ Church University, before his move to his current position at Edge Hill University. Alongside this, until 2010 he was editor of *Primary Music Today*, a national professional magazine for primary music teachers published by Peacock Press. He also held a position as an external examiner for Exeter University PGCE (primary music specialism) for four years. He has continued this role as external examiner since 2013 at the Institute of Education, London, for the primary PGCE programme. He has worked on the Teachers TV Professional Lecture Series, 'What kind of teacher do you want to be?', and is currently a member of the editorial board of the *British Journal of Music Education*.

Since 2010 Ian has been a curriculum designer and training provider, on behalf of Cambridge International Examinations, for music education ITT within the Nile Egyptian Schools Project. His academic research develops his expertise in primary music education, the creative arts and creative pedagogies, and critical policy analysis. His research explores education as well as music, the arts and the primary school, and their relationship. In 2004 his research ability led to him becoming project manager for the Canterbury HEARTS (Higher Education, Arts and Schools) project, which was funded by the Esmee Fairbairn, Paul Hamlyn and Gulbenkian Foundations. The results of his extensive research can be found in the numerous works he has had published.

Cait Talbot-Landers   Cait Talbot-Landers' academic qualifications include BA (Hons) History, MA in History and a PGCE in Primary Education with a specialism in History. In addition, she has an Advanced Certificate in Teaching Primary Geography, an Advanced Study in Teaching Primary Art & Design, as well as the Isle of Man Teaching ICT in Primary School Advanced Level. She is currently studying for a PhD.

Cait has demonstrated a variety of skills throughout her career in school and in higher education. She has been module leader since 2008 for primary and early years Learning Outside the Classroom (LOtC) modules at both undergraduate and postgraduate level, as well as co-module leader for creative and expressive arts. She has also been involved in numerous other projects related to museum education and learning outside the classroom. She was project manager for Museum Placements for Initial Teacher Education, and project managed the EHU and MAGPIE Project, and the Edge Hill's Partnership Development with Schools Project. Cait was a member of the NW Renaissance Steering Committee for ITE and Museums between 2008 and 2011. Alongside her academic positions, she has also been joint coordinator for the National Gallery Associate Partners (Liverpool), for the Cultural Placement Projects, since 2007. Her involvement in a wide range of projects and roles has allowed Cait to develop a number of areas of expertise in relation to LOtC and museum education.

Maggie Webster   Maggie started her NQT career in East London and during this time she was an RE and collective worship coordinator, and a member of Newham's SACRE. She then became a bilingual support teacher, where she was required to work with a variety of teachers and help them adapt their planning to be able to support early stages of English.

In 2000 she became a project manager and museum educator for the British Library (the largest museum library in the UK), where she managed a DfES-funded project called 'Words Alive!'. Maggie's focus was to explore the collection to create thematic and cross-curricular literacy activities, which she then tested with eight schools in Camden and seven schools in Torbay. Later she became a literacy consultant for St Helens Education Action Zone, and worked with three secondary schools and thirteen primary schools developing cross-curricular projects, which encouraged creative thinking in literacy lessons.

Maggie has a BEd (Hons) in Theology and Religious Studies and an MA in Religious Education. She now works as a senior lecturer in primary education at Edge Hill University and is the subject leader for primary religious education. She has presented her work on religious education at numerous conferences and published a selection of papers. She has also presented her work on religion within social media at international conferences in Brno and Salzburg. She has published two books with Pearson Education, presented a lecture on Teachers TV about English as an additional language, and is currently doing a PhD in religious and spiritual expression within social networking spaces.

Preface

We have noticed that, on occasion, trainee teachers find it difficult to understand the link between what they learn and do in university and what they learn and do in school. They seem to value and understand the importance of their professional placements but reflecting on theory and pedagogy can, for some, seem irrelevant. This book therefore aims to bridge this gap so that trainee teachers begin to see how the partnership between school and university is beneficial to them becoming an 'Outstanding' teacher.

The three-lens approach is a framework that has been designed to make explicit the activities teachers do with their class, and the relationship they have with theoretical and pedagogical concepts. The approach has three categories – Identity, Pedagogy and Toolkit – and it can help teachers, teacher trainers and trainee teachers understand what the foundation subjects are, and how to plan, assess and teach them. The approach also provides some creative activity ideas that can be adapted to use for a selection of primary classes that are underpinned by the pedagogy and identity of the discipline. The chapters have been written by specialists in their field who train teachers on a daily basis in university and in school. The approach has been tried and tested within our sessions, so we know it works!

Whatever your reason for picking up this book, we hope it will help you understand the value the foundation subjects can bring to children's holistic development, and enable you to reflect on why and how teachers should continue to teach them in a creative, imaginative and inspirational way.

If you teach them to be average, they'll be average. If you teach them to be good, they'll be good. If you teach them to be themselves, they will be amazing.

Acknowledgements

We would like to thank our final-year trainee teacher Greg Marley for the original artwork he produced for this book. Although a science specialist, he is also an artist – demonstrating, we hope, why we should not restrict the curriculum we give our children and trainees.

Thank you to Stuart Rayner for the photograph on the front cover, of 'Holi: the Celebration of Colour' held at Edge Hill University in 2013 (www.stuartrayner.com).

We also thank the creators of www.Churchads.net and www.christmasstartswith-christ.com for their permission to reproduce three of their many advertisements about Christmas and religion, and Carys Brown for permission to reproduce her late husband's artwork 'Scratcher'.

1 Introduction

Maggie Webster and Sarah Misra

There has been much recent debate about the value of pedagogy versus practice in Initial Teacher Training (ITT) with some key policy makers arguing for school-based apprentice-ship models with increased practical and reduced theoretical content. Routes into teacher training, such as school-centred initial teacher training (SCITT) and School Direct, now vie with more traditional undergraduate and postgraduate teacher training models. Yet, to be a truly excellent teacher who enjoys the profession enough to stay longer than the statistics note (Burns 2012), a teacher needs to develop a balance between the skills needed to prac-tise the craft of teaching and the knowledge and understanding needed to teach effectively. For many primary practitioners, this move towards skills-based teaching is a serious con-cern as there is much research to show that excellence in teacher training programmes is likely to be characterised by a good balance of both practice and pedagogy.

The Donaldson Review (2011: 4) clearly states that teacher education 'requires a more integrated relationship between theory and practice'. Understanding the relation-ship between learning activities for the classroom and pedagogy, the art and science of teaching, will enable practitioners to develop an expertise and understanding of how their teaching can best impact children's learning. Many other educational researchers would concur. Lam and Fung (2001: 12), for example, argue that teaching should be 'intelligent and critical, and accordingly teacher education has to foster such capacities through the-oretical understanding and practical experience'. McLaughlin (1994) also claims that an ability to apply professional knowledge to practice is dependent upon a requirement to develop a deeper understanding of underlying principles and causes through pedagogy.

Reflective teaching

It is important to question the value of teaching pedagogy alongside the more practi-cal aspects of teacher training, and perhaps the most useful concept is the notion of the teacher as a reflective practitioner. There is an increasing emphasis on reflection and the development of reflective practitioners in professional practice (see, for example, Pollard 1987; Grigg 2010; Donaldson 2011) and, during the last decade, reflection has become a basic concept in teacher education all over the world (Pring 2005; Cautreels 2008).

It is clear that teacher education can be delivered using simple technical strategies, but such an overly simplistic approach is damaging to the profession (Loughran 2006). Teachers and children are individuals and each lesson is likely to be influenced by a variety of factors, including the school's ethos, a teacher's philosophy of education and a child's individuality. A reflective teacher who has a range of pedagogies to draw on is more likely to strive to improve their practice and experiment with new strategies, and in turn become an expert teacher rather than simply an experienced practitioner.

Relating theory and practice

When wanting to reflect on and apply pedagogy, trainee teachers seem to value school-based practical experience over opportunities provided by their higher education institu-tions. Hobson *et al.* (2009) found that the majority of their teacher trainees (48 out of 79) stated that their school-based experiences were the most valuable aspect of their initial teacher training.

There seem to be several reasons why many trainees fail to recognise the importance of pedagogical components in their university-based training, namely:

- pedagogy is a complicated business with many definitions;
- the pressures of imminent teaching commitments can restrict opportunity to reflect on pedagogy; in a high-pressure environment, where time is short, it may

be that trainees simply lose patience with the complicated theory and prioritise the actual day-to-day delivery of lessons, while failing to reflect on their effectiveness;

- there are many different approaches to teaching and learning, and no single educational theory can claim to have answers covering all possible challenges; teaching is a complicated business that takes time and patience to craft and perfect.

Some research – such as that of Tann (1994) and Robinson (1993) – also suggests that the ability to reflect on teaching and refine alternative pedagogies is a developmental stage of being a teacher. Trainee teacher needs are often a matter of survival, and they need to be settled and confident in their role before they have enough headspace and experience to reflect on why certain pedagogies work or don't work. Essentially, they must learn to teach before they can reflect upon it.

The three-lens approach

The three-lens model is an attempt to bridge the gap between thorny, complicated pedagogies and skills-based teaching. It has been developed by experienced primary experts who remember the realities and challenges of starting out as primary school teachers. Its structure helps teachers who are new to the profession to understand the relationship between subject identity, pedagogy and teaching tips (which we call toolkit). Simply focusing on toolkit can make lessons become gimmicky, resulting in little impact on children's learning. To become an inspirational, outstanding teacher, it's important to see the value of effective, thoughtful, reflective practice.

The three-lens model is divided into three parts (Figure 1.1).

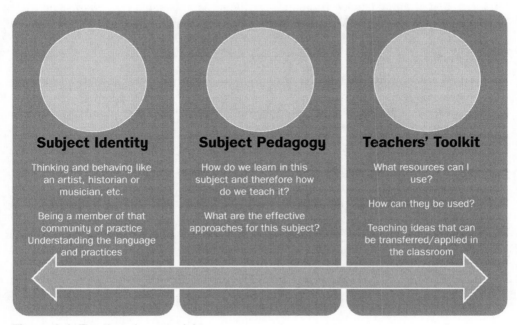

Figure 1.1 The three-lens model

Subject identity

The primary curriculum consists of a selection of subjects that are divided into core (literacy, numeracy and science) and foundation subjects. The term 'foundation subjects' unites many separate disciplines under one umbrella, so it is essential therefore to consider and understand the unique nature or essence of each discipline, or its 'subject-ness', what makes the subject what it is. Under the heading of subject identity we may consider, say, the purpose of a subject, explore technical vocabulary, note how children learn experientially, understand how to behave and act as musicians, historians, artists, etc. Subject identity encourages a teacher to consider the essence of a discipline so that a child is provided with opportunities that enrich their lives and enable them to become rounded individuals.

Curriculum is a subset of the Identity lens. It is important to be aware of what is taught within the discipline because this can frame the distinctive nature of the subject. For example, if the curriculum for religious education was purely focused on Christian or Islamic interpretations of the world it would be fair to say that teachers and pupils may end up with a narrow view of the value religion has for society and the world.

Pedagogy

The term pedagogy – the theory of teaching or how to teach the subject – encompasses a diversity of definitions, understandings and interpretations. Kessels and Korthagen (2001) explore the notion that pedagogy is episteme and phronesis: episteme is 'theory with a big T', and explores large ideas and concepts, and phronesis is 'theory with a small t', which is based on experience and skills (Loughran 2006: 63). Loughran (2006: 11) suggests that, if initial teacher training is 'to do more than simply convey tips and tricks about practice', then we must provide trainee teachers with the opportunity to reflect on their teaching. So it is important to consider the following.

- *What?* What you do and why you do it.
- *So what?* Why is what you do important and what is the impact on children's learning?
- *What now?* What can you do to make it even better so the impact is larger and ensures holistic development?

This book defines pedagogy as the art and science of teaching, and so the sections within the chapters may focus on the theory of planning and how to plan, theory of specific skills related to the discipline and their impact on your teaching, the theory of assessment and how to assess using a curriculum overview, how to structure lessons so that key skills are developed, how to teach creatively within the discipline, etc. Each discipline has a different pedagogy, yet there are some similarities that provide an awareness of the collective identity and pedagogies of the foundation subjects.

Toolkit

The toolkit section is essentially a bank of ideas that can be adapted for use in a primary classroom. As mentioned previously, this is the aspect that most trainee teachers appreciate but, without understanding how it links with identity and pedagogy, it becomes a one-off lesson or project with no real educational value or impact. It can become a 'wow' lesson for an observation but has little impact on the children's understanding of the discipline. Yet toolkit is still an important element of the three-lens model because, without it, teachers may find it difficult to understand what a creative PE lesson might look like or how to teach music musically.

What are the foundation subjects?

The identity of the foundation subjects

The National Curriculum is divided into core subjects and non-core subjects, and the majority of curriculum time is allocated to what are considered to be the basics of a child's education. This stems from the Education Act of 1944 (sometimes called the Butler Act) where, for the first time, legislation stated the legal entitlement a child had to a basic education, namely reading, writing, arithmetic and religious instruction. Since then we have had many curriculum reviews and yet it still stands that the basic curriculum (the core curriculum) should be English, mathematics and science, and the National Curriculum provides detailed guidance for these subjects. As a consequence many schools across the country spend 50 per cent of their daily curriculum time on two of these subjects and 50 per cent on the rest. By default this implies that the remaining subjects are not core to a child's basic education, even though they are valuable enough to be in the National Curriculum. It is therefore ironic when they are bunched together and referred to as 'foundation', which suggests they are fundamental to a child's learning.

Indeed those of us who teach the foundation subjects would say they are the bedrock of a child's development because, collectively, they promote social, emotional, physical, personal, cultural, moral, spiritual and academic skills, and all of the multiple intelligences identified by Howard Gardner (2011). However, they have less curriculum time and in some cases are not taught effectively, if at all, possibly due to a teacher's confidence and the lack of opportunity to teach them, and hence improve practice through reflection.

The foundation subjects have traditionally consisted of six disciplines:

1. art
2. design & technology
3. geography
4. history
5. music
6. physical education.

Religious education is identified as a core subject in faith schools but is a foundation subject in community schools. It is statutory, but what is taught is identified in the local authority syllabus and not in the National Curriculum. Yet, in recent times, other disciplines have been introduced into the National Curriculum under the 'foundation subjects' or 'non-core subjects' umbrella, and have therefore had to have been acknowledged by teachers and training providers. Computing and languages (formally information communication technology and modern foreign languages) are now part of the National

Curriculum and therefore need to be taught in primary classrooms. This has caused trepidation for some teachers because of their lack of experience with such disciplines. Time will tell whether confidence and competence in these disciplines changes, yet due to the limited opportunity to teach such disciplines and reflect on action, it seems that (similar to the other foundation subjects) this is unlikely.

It is essential, therefore, that teachers develop their understanding of the disciplines and reflect on the value the foundation subjects bring to the curriculum so that they make the most of the limited curriculum time available.

The pedagogy of the foundation subjects

For each discipline the general theme within the National Curriculum seems to be that the teacher is the master of the subject and they decide the content. For example, they can decide in languages which modern foreign or ancient foreign language they wish to teach, and in design & technology they choose the theme and product that the children will make. Additionally it is useful to note that the National Curriculum is also not prescriptive of the way you should teach each discipline. Again this is up to the individual teacher and school. This exciting opportunity allows teachers the freedom to experiment and play with various styles of teaching and approaches. However, such flexibility can be daunting for some teachers, who may feel unconfident teaching all or some of the disciplines of the foundation subjects.

This book should be able to help them in some way towards understanding the pedagogy of how to teach these disciplines through acknowledging them as a collective group, and possibly to see some of the similarities, mainly creativity, experiential learning and cross-curricular learning.

Creativity in the foundation subjects

There are many definitions of what the concept of 'creativity' is. Ken Robinson suggests that it is 'divergent thinking', i.e. having original ideas and seeing lots of answers to a question or problem. He argues that as a child grows they are educated out of thinking creatively because the education system narrows their opportunities to think (see RSA Animate – Changing Education Paradigms, online at https://www.youtube.com/watch?v=zDZFcDGpL4U), so teachers need to provide opportunities for children to be creative and learn creatively. The foundation subjects use this concept as a premise for their learning and teaching. Its philosophy is to provide children with opportunities to be creative, i.e. demonstrate what they know, understand and can do, in ways that they choose, and to learn creatively in an environment that fosters personalised learning and individuality (Webster 2010: 21).

Creativity, however, is also an approach. The foundation subjects provide children with the opportunity to be creative by encouraging them to learn and express themselves in ways that are in addition to writing and speaking. For example, children learn through group work, being physical, having individual choice, and with the arts such as music, dance and drama. Much of this learning is conducted in traditional classrooms and school halls, yet the foundation subjects also enjoy exploring key skills through learning outside the classroom (LOtC) in places such as outdoor education centres, in forests, museums, galleries, places of worship, theatres, and so on (see Chapter 11).

The pedagogy of creativity is worth researching further so that you maximise your understanding, because although it is ideal for the foundation subjects, it is also a concept that is considered within all curriculum subjects.

Experiential learning and the foundation subjects

Experiential learning enables children and adults to learn a concept through experiencing something significant, and many of the disciplines within the foundation subjects offer this as a pedagogical tool. Authors have suggested that children learn because there is a purpose to what they are doing and it involves some form of emotional attachment. Teachers have acknowledged this approach to learning and some have included it as a learning approach in addition to the VAK(e) model that has been in favour in recent years, and which is loosely based on Howard Gardner's Multiple Intelligence Theory (Gardner 2011).

In the foundation subjects children may experience being artists, musicians or historians by engaging with artefacts and making music and art. In geography they may explore their local environment and problem solve using maps; in PE they experience the physical aspects of the subject by actually doing it; in RE they may explore the numinous through exploring a sacred space; and in languages they may experience the culture of France through tasting French food and using vocabulary related to a cafe. The experience is an important mode for developing the key skills of each discipline.

Experiential learning requires the teacher to be brave because it is child-led and there are many things that cannot be controlled. It is essentially a socially constructive pedagogy and requires lots of careful planning beforehand so that the children develop deep learning based on the key skills and don't simply remember the experience because it was different. Through scaffolding, teachers can support children's understanding of the learning objective so that the experience offers an enriched, productive outcome that is connected to the discipline(s).

Cross-curricular teaching

Cross-curricular teaching is often confused with thematic learning, yet there is a subtle difference. Cross-curricular teaching is where two or three subjects are taught simultaneously and they drive the lesson, whereas thematic or topic teaching is where one subject is taught and is the driver but the theme/topic links to other curriculum subjects. Cross-curricular teaching is similar to a tandem bicycle: there are two seats and both move the lesson (the bike) forwards. Thematic teaching, therefore, would be a single bicycle, but one that is connected to buggies (the subjects that link).

Over the years, a selection of texts have been published that have promoted thematic and cross-curricular teaching, such as the *Excellence and Enjoyment* document (DfES 2003) and *The Futures Programme: Meeting the Challenge* (DfES 2005). They note that its value is that it relates to the holistic way a child views the world and that it is a good method of covering the National Curriculum in an efficient way.

Some foundation subjects naturally work well together, such as geography and history (sometimes called the humanities), whereas others are more suitable alone, such as gymnastics in physical education, however languages and computing are capable of crossing all boundaries and are able to work with all of the disciplines. There is a danger, however, with cross-curricular teaching in that it can occasionally water down the subject identity of the discipline (Barnes 2012). It is essential therefore that, when teaching in a cross-curricular context, teachers plan objectives for both subjects and also build in assessment opportunities for both, otherwise the enthusiasm for one may overtake the other. Teaching thematically does not have this danger as the teacher is planning and assessing for one discipline while linking to others (Webster 2010).

The structure of this book

This book is divided into a further nine chapters, one for each of the foundation subjects, and a final chapter that explores how to teach the foundation subjects curriculum outside of the classroom, using museums, galleries, archives and the 'outdoors'. Each chapter uses the three-lens model as a framework that explores the relationship between subject identity, pedagogy and toolkit.

Each chapter starts with an overview of the curriculum related to the subject and is directly related to the Primary National Curriculum and syllabi. It continues to explore the unique identity of that particular foundation subject and offers some understanding into the discipline's purpose and value to a child's holistic development. The third main section in each chapter explores various pedagogies related to that discipline, such as how to plan for history, key skills in RE or the process of using sketchbooks in art, whereas the final section offers ideas for the creative teacher's toolkit. The activities in these sections are occasionally structured around a project, such as with design & technology, art and geography, or a selection of ideas such as religious education, music, computing, languages and history.

As being reflective on and in practice is an important part of becoming an outstanding teacher, we have ensured that reflection points are embedded throughout the chapters, and the final summary provides a list of bullet points to help you remember the essential concepts that have been raised.

We trust that this book will be useful before and after qualifying as a primary teacher, and that it will guide you towards understanding the immense value the foundation subjects can bring to children's holistic development. We also hope that you will use it to enthuse and inspire you so that you teach all disciplines in a creative and imaginative way.

References

Barnes, J. (2012) An introduction to cross-curricular learning. In Driscoll, P., Lambirth, A. and Roden, J. (eds) *The Primary Curriculum: A Creative Approach.* London: Sage Publications Ltd, pp. 235–254.

Burns, J. (2012) Numbers of teachers who quit 'up by a fifth' in a year. BBC News, 3 December.

Cautreels, P. (2008) A common emphasis in teacher education and the professional development of teachers: reflection by the teacher. Teacher Education Facing the Intercultural Dialogue, 33rd Conference of the Association for Teacher Education in Europe, Vrije Universiteit, Brussels, 23–27 August.

Department for Education and Skills (DfES) (2003) *Excellence and Enjoyment: A Strategy for Primary Schools.* London: DfES.

Department for Education and Skills (DfES) (2005) *The Futures Programme: Meeting the Challenge.* London: DfES.

Donaldson, J. (2011) Teaching Scotland's future – report of a review of teacher education in Scotland (Donaldson Review). Edinburgh: Scottish Government.

Gardner, H. (2011) *Frames of the Mind: The Theory of Multiple Intelligences.* London: Basic Books.

Grigg, R. (2010) *Becoming an Outstanding Primary School Teacher.* London: Routledge.

Hobson, A.J., Malderez, A., Tracey, L., Giannakaki, M.S., Pell, R.G., Kerr, K., Chambers, G.N., Tomlinson, P.D. and Roper, T. (2009) *Becoming a Teacher: Student Teachers' Experiences of Initial Teacher Training in England.* Nottingham: DfES.

Kessels, J. and Korthagen, F. (2001) The relationship between theory and practice. In Korthagen, F. *et al.* (eds) *Linking Practice and Theory: The Pedagogy of Realistic Teacher Education.* New Jersey: Lawrence Erlbaum Associate.

Lam, J. and Yan Fung, M. (2001) Strengthening teacher training programs: revamping the model of teaching practice. Paper presented at the 2nd Hong Kong Conference on Quality in Teaching and Learning in Higher Education, Hong Kong, May.

Loughran, J. (2006) *Developing A Pedagogy of Teacher Education.* London: Routledge.

McLaughlin, M. (1994) *Rebuilding Teacher Professionalism.* Buckingham: Open University Press.

Pollard, A. (1987) *Ideology and Control in Teacher Education: a Review of Recent Experience in England.* Lewes: Falmer Press.

Pring, R. (2005) *Philosophy of Education: Aims, Theory, Common Sense and Research.* London: Continuum.

Robinson, E. (1993) *Problem Based Methodology: Research for the Improvement of Practice.* London: Sage.

Tann, A. (1994) *Reflective Teaching in the Primary Schools. A Handbook for the Classroom.* Wiltshire: Redwood Books.

Webster, M. (2010) *Creative Approaches to Teaching Primary RE.* Essex: Pearson Education Limited.

2 Art & design

Sarah Misra

One of the greatest privileges of being a primary school teacher is that you get to be a part of the learning journey for each child that you teach. For all children, art & design is a natural form of expression, which supports them in exploring, investigating and communicating their expanding world. Hallam, Das Gupta and Lee (2008) define creativity and expression as vital parts of child development to be recognised, valued and supported, and the creative dimensions that art & design can bring are beneficial to children's learning and growth in countless ways.

> Art is a unique way of knowing and understanding the world. Purposeful visual arts activities expand children's ways of exploring, expressing and coming to terms with the world they inhabit in a structured and enjoyable way.
>
> (NCCA 1999: 2)

Primary-age children in particular are often enviably natural, uninhibited and free in their explorations. All human beings, but especially children, are 'inventive, creative beings who naturally involve themselves in artistic enterprise in order to make sense of increasingly complex worlds' (Key and Stillman 2009), testing out materials and techniques to see what they will do, and communicating through visual and tactile means, with or without the intervention of teachers.

Art & design is also something that young children tend to naturally enjoy (Tutchell 2014) and therefore those who teach it can generally count on an audience who are keen to take part. There is an inherent need within children to draw on a steamed-up window or build sandcastles on a beach. At school, this natural inclination should be built upon, expanded and developed, and it is the responsibility of the teacher to provide as many opportunities as possible to inspire, encourage and ignite the visual and tactile imaginations of the young children that they teach.

> Children see before they speak, make marks before they write, build before they walk. But their ability to appreciate and interpret what they observe, communicate what they think and feel, or make what they imagine and invent, is influenced by the quality of their art, craft and design education.
>
> (Ofsted 2012)

Given the contribution that art & design makes to the education of children and consequently its impact on the lives of adults, it must always be an essential part of the curriculum in primary schools. Taught in the right way, art & design can open up possibilities for a lifetime of artistic enterprise and a love of creativity with all the associated joy and opportunity that this can bring.

The identity of art & design

The next section will deal with the nuts and bolts of the requirements of the National Curriculum – 'what is to be taught' – but we should first ask, 'Why teach it?' This part of the chapter will look at the role that art & design plays in the primary curriculum and, in particular, its value as a subject.

The Arts Council's website states that:

> The arts fuel children's curiosity and critical capacity. They are every child's birthright. It is vital that children engage with the arts early in their lives. The arts contribute to the development and wellbeing of children and young people. They inspire future audiences and the next generation of artists and arts leaders.

The acquisition of a wide and extensive range of new skills accrued by children in art & design lessons is, in itself, a very important reason to teach the subject, but the benefits of an artistic education extend much further than this.

Young children tend to feel positive about art & design. They are usually willing to have a go. Ask a class of five year olds 'Who can draw?' and they will often all raise their hands. Ask the same question to high-school children and you are likely to get a very different response. Most young children will relish the freedom and creativity of art, but as children mature they become increasingly aware of their likes and dislikes, make judgements about their abilities and develop a feeling of what they are 'good at'.

Although certain children will have more of a natural flair for art & design than others, it is important to consider the range of needs in your classroom, and cultivate a shared, supportive ethos around a commitment to the belief that each child has the potential to progress their own personal creativity and artistic development. There are many ways to do this, such as providing opportunities to work collaboratively, setting activities that develop the imagination, encouraging experimental approaches, focusing on process rather than outcome, and providing opportunities for exploration of techniques and materials. These approaches will ensure that all children can achieve.

Art & design is traditionally a subject where all children can achieve. It is a subject that helps them to make valuable creative links, solve problems and to use their brain in a distinctive way; because of this it has been shown to have a positive effect both on those who enjoy and achieve highly in academic tasks and those who may not. All children should have equal access to visual arts education. Avoid grouping children in terms of their academic ability; instead take time to assess their artistic ability and differentiate the skills and complexity of activities to develop ability, building on earlier experiences and skills acquired. This is often seen by teachers as more difficult in the foundation subjects, however the principle is the same as in any other subject.

Art & design has the potential to be a truly inclusive subject where all children can achieve. There are limitless opportunities for teachers to provide opportunities for their pupils to develop a positive awareness of different cultures and traditions. Valuing diversity and individuality is what the subject is all about. However it is also worth noting that Ofsted states that the national gap between high achievement of boys and girls is bigger in art & design than in any other subject, with boys falling behind. Plan for activities that will appeal to boys as well; they have many role models in the art world.

Art & design topics that relate to children's personal experiences, feelings and observations allow occasions for them to develop valuable communication skills, realising a vital human need to express emotions. Primary-aged children's growing awareness of themselves, their relationships with friends and family, and interaction with their world provides opportunities for self-exploration, and can stimulate meaningful and profound work. Combining specific learning with pupils' personal and wider experiences offers opportunities to promote spiritual, moral, social and cultural development through artistic enterprise.

The subject of art & design also enables the development of cultural knowledge and capabilities, giving children and young people opportunities to recognise, appreciate and enjoy practical art activity and design skills, develop intellectual and aesthetic awareness, and to foster a critical response to artists' work. Children articulate their own ideas and develop the ability to make critical judgements. It is important to plan carefully for opportunities for children to familiarise themselves with other artistic spaces such as local gallery displays, museums and exhibitions. These experiences enrich pupils' knowledge of the arts, allowing for involvement in creative activities in real settings. Many local events may also strengthen understanding of local heritage, impacting positively on their sense of belonging. Experiencing the arts in this way has been shown to have a beneficial impact on pupils' learning, both in art, craft and design, and on their broader confidence and aesthetic development.

Art & design activities should allow children to develop their own thinking and questioning skills, and promote innovation, risk taking and problem solving. In a world that is changing faster than ever before, these are hugely valuable skills, teaching them to be flexible, adaptable and resilient. Art is a great subject for learning about resilience as any creative process inevitably involves mistakes. Let the children feel safe to make mistakes and let them see you make mistakes too – it's a great opportunity to teach them that failure isn't final but a vital part of the learning process.

Reflection points

- *What makes art & design distinct from other subjects?*
- *What is the value of art & design as a subject?*

The art & design curriculum

As a primary school teacher, you will need to familiarise yourself with the National Curriculum in order to be compliant with statutory requirements. However, school communities should and do interpret the curriculum in different ways, in order to make them relevant and useful in terms of local interest and available expertise, and the curriculum is purposely written in an open-ended way precisely to encourage this. There is also little in the curriculum that defines the minimum subject entitlement. Because it is not explicitly stated, schools have the freedom to decide what they choose to teach and what resources and time they devote to it.

Curriculum aims

The current National Curriculum retains the fundamental conceptual framework of previous versions. These are given as four 'aims', and children should be given opportunities to:

- produce creative work, exploring their ideas and recording their experiences
- become proficient in drawing, painting and sculpture (and possibly other art, craft and design techniques)
- evaluate and analyse creative works using the language of art, craft and design
- know about 'great' artists, craft makers and designers, and understand the historical and cultural development of their art forms.

Subject content

Defined subject content is minimal. For Key Stage 1, content is defined in simple terms in order to reflect the nature of learning in art for this age range, characterised by open-ended exploration. For Key Stage 2, content progresses to reflect the natural characteristics of children of this age, where developing 'technical skills', 'getting it right' and 'mastery' become more important. Guidance can be broadly divided into three areas, as described below.

Technical knowledge

In terms of materials, Key Stage 1 pupils are simply encouraged to regularly try out as many new materials as possible. You may want to audit the materials available in your school, and map out opportunities for children to become familiar with and confident in using as broad a range as possible.

In Key Stage 2 'pupils should be taught to develop their use of materials, with creativity, experimentation and an increasing awareness of different kinds of art, craft and design' (DfE 2013). Having been exposed to a wide variety of materials and developed an understanding of what is available, older primary children are then able to make informed choices about which to use in order to achieve specific effects.

Key Stage 1 children are also required to 'develop a wide range of techniques in using colour, pattern, texture, line, shape, form and space' (DfE 2013). These are the basic elements of a visual language and are defined more extensively in the pedagogy section of this chapter, but it is important that children are given opportunities to explore these elements and put them into practice.

By Key Stage 2, opportunities to move learning on should be planned for as pupils should be taught to develop their techniques, experiment, and build an increasing awareness of different kinds of art, craft and design. They are also required to 'improve their mastery of art & design techniques including drawing, painting and sculpture with a range of materials (for example pencil, charcoal, paint, clay)' (DfE 2013).

Expression

Once again the emphasis in Key Stage 1 is on exposure to opportunities to 'use drawing, painting and sculpture to develop and share their ideas, experiences and imagination' (DfE 2013). In other words, children should use their new-found understanding of materials and techniques to express their ideas. They may look at different collage materials and suggest which would be the most appropriate material and why, they may use paint-mixing techniques to find exactly the right flesh colour, or they may look at different ways to express feelings or light and dark.

In Key Stage 2 these opportunities increase and older primary children should be taught to 'create sketch books to record their observations and use them to review and revisit ideas' (DfE 2013). It is worth emphasising that a 'sketchbook' in this context is not simply a book for sketching; this will be developed in the 'toolbox' section of this chapter.

Appreciation of the work of others

This area requires pupils to develop a working knowledge of artists, craftspeople and designers, and their roles. Children should be able to investigate the work of others to support their own developing artistic activity, develop a visual literacy and growing awareness of the use of visual and tactile elements in art, learn to interpret and respond to works of art, and develop an understanding of art as an expression of historical and cultural context. It is important to ensure that the emphasis of this part of the curriculum is on art as inspiration rather as something to copy, as this will not allow them opportunities to be personally creative or expressive.

At Key Stage 1 the guidance is 'for children to study the work of a range of artists, craft makers and designers, to be able to describe differences and similarities between different practices and disciplines, and to make links to their own work' (DfE 2013). In Key Stage 2 pupils must 'learn about great artists, architects and designers in history' (DfE 2013). The omission of craftspeople from this list should not be taken to indicate that crafts should not feature, as guidance clearly states that children should have an increasing awareness of 'different kinds of art, craft and design'.

Historically, primary schools have been criticised for a tendency to define 'great' artists rather narrowly, and to focus on a fairly predictable range of dominant artists and craftspeople rather than looking to a wider field of expertise in order to provide good role models for previously marginalised demographics. One of the challenges for modern primary school teachers may be to ensure that children's experience of art extends beyond the western classical tradition to include art forms from a range of cultures and times, enabling children to develop increased cultural awareness, sensitivity and appreciation of diversity. Schools are given the freedom to make their art & design curriculum distinct, and have the flexibility to take the individual and unique features of their own communities and local resources into account, helping children to place themselves and to explore their own heritage.

Reflection points

- *What activities would encourage an understanding of the visual elements of colour, pattern, texture, line, shape, form and space?*
- *How could you use the work of artists, designers and craftspeople in your teaching?*

The pedagogy of art & design

There are many different approaches to delivering art & design in primary education; all have their place and stronger arts provision will incorporate more than one approach into their delivery, develop partnerships with other agencies and organisations, and integrate their arts teaching into their particular locality allowing for specific expertise to be exploited fully, and reinforcing pupils' understanding of local heritage and sense of belonging.

Key skills for teaching art & design

Planning

Planning plays as important and valid part in teaching art & design as it does in any subject. Although you may want the outcomes to be more fluid and creative, you will still need to think carefully about how you will provide opportunities for children to stimulate and develop ideas, and how you will support them in bringing these ideas to a final conclusion.

There is no one way of planning for art & design. Different schools will have their own planning structures, and these may or may not be linked to the curriculum, dependent on the status of the school. However, any planning should always be grounded in achievable and challenging objectives: what do I want the children to learn rather than what activity shall we do. When you are identifying learning objectives make sure that these build on existing knowledge, are broken down into small, achievable steps and written in child-friendly language so that children are able to understand what is required of them.

Many successful art & design lessons begin with a stimulus that fires the children's imaginations – this could be in the form of an exciting theme, materials or tools, techniques, others' work or in links made to existing experiences. In most cases – particularly in schools that embrace cross-curricular teaching – you will be adapting your lessons to the school's long-term planning themes.

When you have chosen a theme it is important to think about the medium/media that you want to cover and investigate whether any existing artist's work would be suitable to use in your teaching. Those media specified in the primary curriculum are:

- drawing materials
- painting materials
- sculpture materials

but may also include, among others:

- print-making materials
- collage materials
- textile materials
- digital media
- photographic media
- mixed media.

As the teacher, you should have understanding of the children's prior learning to ensure a breadth of experience and developmental levels so that you can build on these. Skills and techniques to be taught will be dependent on the materials that you have chosen to use. Examples are given in Table 2.1.

Teaching

Guided discovery is an effective teaching method for the visual arts, encouraging children to discover the expressive possibilities of a variety of materials and tools suitable

Table 2.1   Develop knowledge about drawing, painting and sculpture

DRAWING Develop knowledge about...	PAINTING Develop knowledge about...	SCULPTURE Develop knowledge about...
different media, e.g. pencils, charcoals, pastels and how to use them	different paints and how to use them	different media, e.g. clay, modroc, etc., and how to use them
a range of different tools: papers, different pencil grades, rubbers, etc.	a range of different tools: papers, canvas, paintbrushes, etc.	range of different tools used in sculpture
how to create effects such as depth, tone, line, shading using drawing materials	how to create effects such as depth, tone, light (colour mixing, layering, adding water, etc.) using paints	different techniques in clay by making, e.g. thumb pots, coil pots, slab pots
manipulating different drawing materials to create specific effects	manipulating different paints to create specific effects	manipulating different media to create specific effects
measuring and perspective	primary, secondary, tertiary colours (and how to mix them)	specific forming, joining and cutting techniques
how to build compositions from simple shapes	colour theory (relationship between colours, creating mood and feeling with colour)	simple shape and form

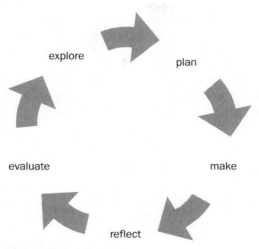

Figure 2.1 Art cycle

for a particular task, and to experiment with them. This discovery may look organic but will need to be carefully planned. Although exploration should be the basis of most art & design lessons, there will also be times when focused teaching, usually through demonstration, is a more appropriate way for children to learn a skill or practise a technique.

The teaching model in Figure 2.1 can be used when planning an art activity, and can also be adapted to the delivery of a unit of work. It allows children the space and time to explore and plan before making or creating a piece of art and also gives opportunities for reflection and evaluation afterwards.

At the beginning of a unit of work the aim is to provide children with opportunities to explore and investigate. This is essential and should always precede making. It can sometimes be a challenge as many children do not want to explore, preferring instead to dive straight in and create their masterpiece.

There are usually lots of opportunities here for using artists' work to support and stimulate learning. Looking at and talking about works of art is a way for children to explore and respond to what they see. It is important that work is used thoughtfully and that children are not expected to simply copy works of art but to explore the main aspects of the artist's work.

Certain practical skills and techniques, such as the use of new materials or tools, will require a more direct method of teaching. When you are introducing or developing a skill or new medium, one of the most effective ways to do this is by demonstrating to the class or to small groups. No matter how straightforward a new project may seem, there is always value in working through it yourself before you teach it, thinking through how to explain each step and what the potential problems might be.

Further demonstration can be given to small groups and individuals to support or extend them further. Working on the children's work should always be avoided! Often children have a tendency to think that the best way to please the teacher is by replicating their example. It is important to enforce that this should be their own work, focusing on the skill or technique rather than the outcome.

Having practised key skills and gained some understanding of the expectations and how to achieve objectives, providing opportunities for the children to explore and talk about ideas in order to plan their own piece of work is fundamental. A common weakness of lessons judged to be only satisfactory by Ofsted is teachers' reluctance to adjust their prepared lesson plan in response to pupils' emerging reactions and ideas. Rigid adherence to a lesson plan will mean that pupils' own creative ideas will not be pursued. Allow them to use their experiences from the explore phase to inform their planning of the making phase.

In the middle of a unit of work you will be planning for the children to use their experiences and inspiration, and to put them into practice. Do you want children to be working collaboratively or individually? Will you allow them to choose how they would like to work? There will be certain success criteria that children must achieve but there should also be scope for personal responses so that you don't end up with 30 identical pieces of work.

Opportunities to stop and reflect should be planned in at each stage to enable children to make decisions and to reflect on the work that they have undertaken. Towards the end of the project, plans should include opportunities for children to talk about the finished piece.

Assessment

Terms such as testing, evaluation and assessment often elicit a negative response when related to creative subjects and there are certainly advocates of art & design teaching who would argue that creative output cannot and should not be assessed. Arguments against assessment include the idea that judgements by others may restrict creativity, may be product rather than process driven and that measuring success is incompatible with the arts.

However, although National Curriculum levels are being abandoned, there is increasing demand for schools to track progress and develop clear assessment criteria. It is important to develop a continuous process of documenting and recording a child's development to enable teachers to make appropriate formative decisions about teaching and learning, to investigate concerns and to inform interventions. Assessment should do more than simply measure. A critical factor of successful teaching is the feedback given to pupils linked to lesson objectives and success criteria. With care and sensitivity it is possible to support the development of the discipline of art design while allowing for personal expression and interpretation.

Reflection points

- *Why is it important to give children opportunities to explore and plan before making?*
- *What is more important – process or outcome? Why?*
- *How can you sensitively and constructively assess art & design in your classroom?*

The art & design teacher's toolkit

This part of the chapter is designed to help teachers to make sense of and to apply the requirements of the art design curriculum in practice. It is important to note that these offerings are purely suggestions and ideas, and do not attempt to propose a definitive list. As discussed, the best teaching is adapted and developed to the pupils' interests, experiences and prior learning.

The seven visual and tactile elements in art & design

The seven visual and tactile elements in art & design as set out in the National Curriculum are space, texture, colour, form, line, pattern and shape (see Table 2.2). A basic understanding of them is essential to purposeful art & design teaching and a developing visual vocabulary and ability to create visually and spatially help children to build their own capacity for artistic expression.

Table 2.2   Seven elements table

SPACE	Definition
	space can be either the creation of the illusion of space and depth on a flat surface or a three-dimensional work
	Key vocabulary
	boundary, border, edge, overlap, negative, positive, gap, hole, aperture, balance, relation, size
	Examples of useful art movements and artists
	De Stijl – Piet Mondrian; surrealism – Rene Magritte; conceptual art – Yayoi Kusama

TEXTURE	Definition
	texture refers to the roughness or smoothness of a surface and is an important aspect of the visual and tactile world. Children need opportunities to explore texture through touch, such as finger painting or manipulating clay, and through looking, talking about and making marks. Opportunities should be provided for them to work on textured surfaces and to discover their own ways of creating a variety of textures
	Key vocabulary
	smooth, rough, impasto, uneven, dull, shiny, course, fine, granulated, matt, gloss, relief, contour
	Examples of useful art movements and artists
	British romanticism – Turner; post-impressionism – Van Gogh; textiles – Lesley Richmond; illustrator – Eric Carle

(Continued)

Table 2.2 Seven elements table *(Continued)*

COLOUR	
Definition	
	Knowledge of colour helps the pupils to understand how it may be used in art & design to create effects such as light, symbolically or to represent emotions. The traditional method of organising and making sense of colours is the colour wheel, which shows relationships between primary colours (red, yellow and blue), secondary colours (those made using two primary colours – orange, purple, green), etc. Temperature in art terms refers to the warm and cool halves of the colour spectrum
Key vocabulary	
	primary, secondary, tertiary colours, colour theory, colour wheel, complementary colours, contrast, harmony, tone, hue, saturation, intensity, monochrome, achromatic, opaque, transparent, translucent, shade, tint, spectrum
Examples of useful art movements and artists	
	Abstract expressionism – Jackson Pollock; impressionism – Claude Monet; colour field painting – Mark Rothko; fauvism – Henri Matisse; Scottish colourists – John Duncan Fergusson; English ceramicist – Clarice Cliff; textile artist – Kaffe Fassett; architect – Friedensreich Hundertwasser

FORM	
Definition	
	In art & design, form is the name given to three-dimensional shape and is solid. Children can experience large-scale forms by moving around them, or smaller forms by picking them up and observing them
Key vocabulary	
	organic, geometric, regular, irregular, weight, mass, balance, structure, space
Examples of useful art movements and artists	
	land art – Andy Goldsworthy, Tim Pugh; modernista architecture – Antoni Gaudi; figurative sculpture – Auguste Rodin, Elisabeth Frink

LINE	
Definition	
	Line is the basic element in children's early mark making and drawing, and helps the artist to define shapes or represent edges. Lines can be used in many ways and do not have to be single continuous marks but can be a series of dashes or dots, and can have their own dimensions including size, direction, length and weight
Key vocabulary	
	straight, curved, fine, thick, thin, wavy, zig-zag, organic, rhythmic, pressure, light, dash, dotted, broken, perspective, proportion, vanishing point, cross-hatching, horizontal, vertical, diagonal
Examples of useful art movements and artists	
	Constructivism – Naum Gabo; futurism – Umberto Boccioni; woodcut book illustrations – Albrecht Durer; linear abstraction – Wassily Kandinsky; illustrator – Lauren Child

Table 2.2 Seven elements table *(Continued)*

	Definition
PATTERN	Wenham (2003) suggests that there are three main types of pattern: linear patterns (developed along a line), rotating patterns (developed around a point) and surface patterns (developed on flat surfaces to cover whole areas). Pattern is the constant repetition of a motif, and can be used to achieve unity, rhythm, variety and movement
	Key vocabulary
	shape, space, design, repeat, print, rotate, motif, sequence, grid, embellish, decorate, mosaic, symmetry
	Examples of useful art movements and artists
	Aboriginal art – Emily Kame Kngwarreye; cubism – Pablo Picasso; vorticism – Helen Saunders; eco art – Andy Goldsworthy; arts & crafts – William Morris; symbolism – Gustav Klimt; textile/ceramics – Orla Kiely; textile artist – Alison Mercer

	Definition
SHAPE	Shape in the context of art is concerned with defining areas on a flat surface, and can be created by identifying an outline with a pen, tearing paper or creating a potato print
	Key vocabulary
	square, circle, oval, triangle, organic, regular, irregular, two-dimensional, three-dimensional, flat, concentric, repeated, rotated, symmetry
	Examples of useful art movements and artists
	cubism – Pablo Picasso; fauvism – Henri Matisse; surrealism – Jean Arp, Salvador Dali; orphism – Sonia Delaunay; optical art – Bridget Riley

Using sketchbooks

The sketchbook is much more than a book with blank paper in to draw on. It allows children to create, imagine, respond, observe, design and record, creating independent and confident artists. One of the most important aspects of using sketchbooks in art & design education is that it encourages children to become more actively involved with their own learning experiences and to enjoy a sense of control, decision making and ownership that can be both empowering and enjoyable. For this to happen it is important that teachers encourage pupils to take ownership of their work, and that they feel safe to experiment and test out ideas. Below are some of the ways that you can use a sketchbook in your classroom.

Explore
Learning to observe detail is an important element of art & design education. Children should be encouraged to develop this skill by studying an object and making investigative sketches.

Through their drawings they are able to gather specific information on how things are made or work.

Develop initial ideas

Rather than being the place for a final, polished piece of work, encourage children to use their sketchbook as an initial way of recording responses to various stimuli, and as a place to practise, develop and focus their ideas. Allow this to be a place where they can make mistakes, acting as a reference point and a resource for future work. It may be useful to date and title work to provide a record for both the teacher and the children themselves.

Acquire skills and techniques

Sketchbooks are great places to practise drawing techniques such as shading, perspective and drawing from different viewpoints, but don't have to be confined to drawing; they could also be used to test out different materials and techniques such as colour mixing or using chalk or oil pastels. As well as the sketch itself the children might record details about the item being drawn or sketched for future reference, and notes on the actual technical processes involved.

Review and modify ideas

Children should be taught that if they decide they are not happy with their work and decide to start again they are reviewing their work and that their subsequent modified attempts will show progress. Sketchbooks can also be used to review and record their thoughts on the artwork that they have produced, identifying positive features and ways in which their work could be developed or improved. Avoiding 'rubbing out' or 'throwing away' the earlier attempts provides the child and the teacher with a method of reviewing what has been done previously.

Respond to other artists and craftspeople

As previously discussed, it is important for the children to gain knowledge and understanding of a variety of artists and craftspeople. The sketchbook can be used to compare works of art, craft and design with children encouraged to write comments and record their own personal reactions and responses to the ideas, methods and approaches of different artists.

Collect information

Although it is important to maintain the identity of the sketchbook (rather than allowing it to become a scrapbook) it can be really useful to collect ideas, information and inspiration, such as:

- photographs
- photocopies from magazines, comics, calendars, artists' work, etc.
- cards, stamps, samples of textures, fabrics and other materials
- poems, stories, titles of music used to stimulate a response
- resources that the children might need to produce a piece of art, mix a colour, etc.
- colour, tone strips from colour mixing.

Starting with an artist/artwork or topic – example artist: William Brown, topic: bears!

Figure 2.2 *Scratcher.*
Source: William Brown

Choosing an artist

Choose an artist who will appeal to the children, fits into your long-term school plan (allowing for a range of experiences) and that you like! William Brown is a great artist to use with primary-age children as his subject matter appeals and he painted in a naive, childlike style, using lots of bright colours that are immediately accessible to children (see Figure 2.2). He also used lots of visual imagery from myths, folklore and poetry, meaning that there are plenty of links to be made with literacy and the children will be exposed to different cultural references.

Week one: explore

Subject content covered: developing technical knowledge/appreciation of the work of others.

Show the children pictures by William Brown on the interactive whiteboard. These might include 'Le Loup Garou' (Leaping Wolf), Trojan Horse or Peek-a-boo Moose, as well as 'Scratcher'. It is important to show more than one so that they can see common features, but not too many as this will become overwhelming. Talk about relevant visual and tactile elements, particularly colour, line, shape, pattern, and ask what they see.

Discuss how William Brown painted: he worked in a studio and painted large-scale pieces of art on to canvas. He used big brushes and acrylic paints to achieve the broad lines and bright colours. There are opportunities here to link to other cultures as William Brown's family originally came from Scotland and have their own McClure tartan, which he incorporated into some of his work (also good for discussion around pattern).

Create opportunities for children to explore the artist through other subject areas – for example, you could look at stories, images or books about wolves, read stories such as 'Little Red Riding Hood' or practise moving like a wild animal in the forest.

Weeks two and three: plan
Subject content covered: developing technical knowledge, expression, appreciation of the work of others.

At this point I like to give children a brief, and determine success criteria so that they understand exactly what they are required to do. In this example I might tell them that they will be creating a painting of their own bear, taking inspiration from William Brown's work. I would work with the children to negotiate requirements: give it a name, make it large scale, use vivid colours and patterns like William Brown, etc.

Before children can plan their work, they need to develop some skills. Spend time allowing the children to develop technical knowledge by experimenting with different materials, mixing paints, wax crayons, shiny papers, etc. Children can find out how these can be applied and what the different effects are. Use mark making to experiment on sheets of paper and a variety of sizes and types of paintbrushes in different ways. This is a good place to use some key vocabulary such as intensity of colour, hue, depth, etc.

You may wish to provide an opportunity here for children to develop their observational skills and to use their sketchbooks to make observational drawings of soft bears in order to investigate the shape of a bear, or to practise drawing large-scale pictures working in pairs or groups to develop patterns and colours. Remember to demonstrate and model key skills to the children and then to challenge them to find other methods. Support children in refining their plans ready for the make activity.

Weeks four and five: make
Subject content covered: developing technical knowledge, expression, appreciation of the work of others.

Children can now develop their investigations into a final piece of work. Think about how you want the children to work – individually or in groups to develop skills of collaboration and negotiation. Ensure that children have space and time to work. Consider how you will deploy adults in the room.

It is often useful before starting to recap on the brief and success criteria, and perhaps to share different ideas from the planning stage, what worked for people and what didn't. It is also important here to discuss the idea of process not product, and to assure children that very few pieces of work will look like they do in their heads!

You will need to plan carefully to allow children access to a range of materials to ensure that they are not confined by limited resources, while ensuring that they use materials and techniques that you want them to develop.

Week six: reflect and evaluate
Subject content covered: developing technical knowledge, expression, appreciation of the work of others.

In this session children should be given a chance to reflect on the creative process, and to consider whether they met the initial brief and achieved the success criteria. Did they achieve the effects that they wanted to, and if not why not? What do they love about their work? How would they change it next time? Note here that it is important to praise and encourage; rather than general positive comments this should be focused, specific and meaningful, and therefore a tool for motivating and learning.

Give children opportunities to consider the work of others and to evaluate in a positive way; options include peer evaluation, whole-class evaluation, etc. It is always nice to create a gallery of work as a celebration of the topic, even to create a gallery open event by inviting parents in and providing drinks and nibbles!

Summary of key points

- Art & design is a fundamental requirement in the primary curriculum, and has value both as a subject and in terms of developing creativity as a skill.
- The art & design curriculum allows considerable freedom but requires children to develop knowledge and understanding of materials and processes, knowledge of the creative process, and knowledge of a range of artists, craftspeople and designers.
- Children should be given opportunities to explore, develop, investigate, make, present, review and evaluate.
- The seven key visual and tactile elements in art & design are colour, pattern, texture, line, shape, form and space.
- Sketchbooks are beneficial and can be used in many ways.

References

Cox, S. and Watts, R. (2007) *Teaching Art & Design 3–11*. New York: Continuum.

Department for Education (DfE) (2013) *The National Curriculum for England Framework Document*. London: DfE.

Hallam, J., Das Gupta, M. and Lee, H. (2008) An exploration of primary school teachers' understanding of art and the place of art in the primary school curriculum. *Curriculum Journal*, 19, 4, pp. 269–281.

Key, P. and Stillman, J. (2009) *Teaching Primary Art & Design*. Exeter: Learning Matters.

NCCA (1999) *Visual Arts, Arts Education Teacher Guidelines*. Dublin: Government Publications.

Ofsted (2012) *Making a Mark: Art, Craft and Design Education 2008–11*. London: Ofsted.

Tutchell, S. (2014) *Young Children as Artists: Art & Design in the Early Years and Key Stage 1*. London: Routledge.

Wenham, M. (2003) *Understanding Art: A Guide for Teachers*. London: Sage Publications.

3 Computing

Chris Russell

It can be argued that the biggest change to primary schools, and their curriculum, has taken place in the field of what was formerly known as ICT. Re-branded for a new generation, ICT has shaken off its shackles and regenerated. ICT (information and communication technologies) implies, in its name, the generality of information to be shared and observed. Computing now firmly falls under the foundation umbrella and has a focus not only on the outcomes that can be achieved with the use of technology, but also the process of coding, control and programming, making it relevant and immediate.

At least, that's what a first glance at the curriculum would suggest. If we dig a little further, the elements of previous curriculums are still evident. Children are still required to master skills associated with word processing, art packages and media work. However, they are now also required to 'design, write and debug programs' as well as to 'explain how some simple algorithms work'. This can be seen as an extension of work children have previously known as control and making things happen.

Traditionally, ICT has been a subject that terrifies and excites in equal measure. Some teachers thrive on new technologies and the endless possibilities that are presented, while others retreat, disengage and yearn for simpler times. The curriculum that was presented in 2013 for implementation in September 2014 sparked the imagination of teachers who recognised that projects, skills and understanding associated with the old curriculum had become stale, outdated and unchallenging.

A move towards a curriculum concerned with the creation of apps, coding and uses of applications such as MITT's 'Scratch' was welcomed by many as a way of reinvigorating lessons that involved technology. This was, for many, a natural move forward for the curriculum. It would help prepare children for the technologically advanced world that awaits them once they leave school.

Equally, children brought up on X-box and PlayStation games, with their sophisticated graphics and processor speeds, will be able to see stronger links between the tasks they complete in their computing lessons and the real world. Engagement and motivation are addressed as children will move away from repetitive – and arguably pointless – tasks, towards creating content that will inspire them and a new generation.

Perhaps the most proactive statement to be found in the curriculum document that was released in September 2013, and one that outlines the new direction for the 2014 curriculum, is a line that asserts that, 'The core of computing is computer science', adding that children are 'to be taught the principles of information and computation, how digital systems work and how to put this knowledge to use through programming'. Given that the terms 'computing' and 'computer science' are new to primary schools, this is quite a statement of intent.

The identity of computing

The bespoke nature of computing is harder to pinpoint than other more traditional, foundation subjects such as history or art. Computing tends to adapt to the needs of the children at each particular school or setting, and to be determined by the facilities, resources and expertise on hand to deliver it.

However, Allen *et al.* (2012) have identified a number of key characteristics of computing as a teaching and learning strategy, which goes some way towards revealing the identity of computing. Allen *et al.* (2012) highlight the importance of teachers making 'informed decisions' about the use of technology and the way in which it is used in the classroom.

The first key feature of computing that is identified by Allen *et al.* (2012) is that of interactivity. Interactivity can be experienced in a number of ways through the use of technology. The immediacy of feedback is highlighted as being particularly engaging and useful in developing learning, whether it is the results of a search or the formation of a graph or simulation on screen. The role of the teacher in such learning activities remains of the utmost importance, and the level of interaction between pupil and teacher depends upon the way in which the teacher has designed each learning activity. Allen *et al.* (2012: 9) highlight the role of the teacher as 'encouraging the children to explore', 'to develop perseverance in trying out ideas'. They also emphasise the importance of 'learning from feedback' as this is 'vital in maximising the educational value of the experience for the children'.

Another key characteristic of computing is that of provisionality. Provisionality allows children to make changes to their work and to try out things without having a detrimental impact upon their final work. This sense of security allows for a greater development of ideas and a willingness to ask 'what if?' questions. The key feature of provisionality straddles all aspects of children's work with computers, from word processing and text-based editing to the computing aspect of coding and control technologies. Allen *et al.* (2012) see the teacher's role at this stage as fostering 'positive attitudes' towards provisionality, as well as encouraging discussion, reflection and encouraging the children to review their work.

Allen *et al.* (2012) also talk about computing in terms of capacity and range. 'Capacity and range' refers to the array of digital information that can be accessed in a variety of different forms, whether that be text, images or sound. Capacity and range also refers to 'the modes by which information is communicated' (2012: 9); this includes desktops, PCs, tablets, phones and other devices, some of which may well be described as 'new technologies'. Allen *et al.* (2012) warn that, with this increasing 'multi-modality', children need to be developed in the skills required to deal with such vast amounts of information, including the ability to critically evaluate the provenance of such information, a necessary skill for today's multimedia society.

Speed and automatic function as key characteristics of computing are important as they allow for children to create, capture, store and retrieve information effectively. As a result, users can 'read, observe, interrogate, interpret, analyse and synthesise information at higher levels' (2012: 9). Completing routine procedures at speed allows time for children to consider the implications of the information they are interrogating and the manner in which it has been presented.

By recognising the key features, or characteristics, of computing, teachers can make best use of technology when they plan and design their computing lessons for the children they teach. Therefore, lessons become efficient and effective, and have more of an impact on the children's learning and progress.

An Ofsted report, published in April 2014, indicates aspects of outstanding quality of teaching in computing, stating that teaching should be informed by 'excellent subject knowledge and understanding' (Ofsted 2014). In lessons where teaching was deemed to be outstanding, pupils were engaged and active in 'carefully planned' and 'imaginative lessons'. Misconceptions were addressed effectively, and children were encouraged, challenged and inspired. These statements are not generic level descriptors, but an indication of good practice over a length of time in a range of schools. The same document highlights outstanding achievement of pupils as being 'effective use of a wide range of hardware and software', and 'high levels of originality, imagination, creativity and innovation in their understanding and application of computing skills' (Ofsted 2014).

While some of these statements may appear to be obvious, using a document such as this in addition to section five of the Ofsted Whole School Inspection Framework, and with reference to the key features of computing that have been outlined by Allen *et al.* (2012), teachers can plan and deliver insightful, purposeful teaching and learning experiences that are not only focused on learning but will also meet with Ofsted approval.

The identity of computing as a subject, as highlighted earlier, adapts to the needs and ethos of each school. For instance, many primary schools spent their NGfL money on a suite of computers, while other schools bought trolleys of laptops, and others created communal banks of PCs, rather than whole classrooms. Some schools had already created a clear ideology for the manner in which they were going to deliver lessons using computing. In each instance, the way in which computing was initially implemented in their school will have had a fundamental impact on how the subject has been perceived ever since. This may manifest itself in the way computing has established cross-curricular links with other subjects, or the use of the computing suite and the ease of access to the computers. The way in which the computing suite is managed and booked by individual classes will have an impact on the lessons that are undertaken. Ease of access to the resources has a significant impact upon the way in which computing is embedded in the curriculum of the school.

Schools are constantly adapting their provision of computing, to cater for the latest developments, technologies, thinking and curriculum. Often concern regarding the implementation of computing in schools stems from the thought that use of computers equates to nothing more than an enhanced presentation for the lesson or that use of technology is seen as a glorified computer game or gimmick rather than a legitimate learning experience. The resolution to these questions probably rests with the attitudes of each individual teacher and the way in which technology, or e-learning, is adopted by their school and in their own minds, and essentially how the technology is actually used and implemented.

Often the identity of computing as a subject is clouded by the fact that there has always been a debate among educators as to whether computing is taught discretely in lessons that focus solely on developing skills, knowledge and understanding in aspects of technology, or whether a more cross-curricular approach should be adopted. Discrete teaching of computing could be seen as the accumulation of specific skills related to different types of software and different purposes, resulting in the children's ability to put their new-found skills and understanding into practice in order to produce a designated outcome or achieve a specific goal. This model closely resembles that of the original QCA schemes of work.

However, another approach to the delivery of computing stems from a more amalgamated model, whereby children learn new skills and techniques as and when they require them in order to progress in their learning in other subjects. This is perhaps best demonstrated through the use of branching databases in a science lesson. The children are set the task of classifying and sorting animals or identifying habitats. In this model, the children's computing development would be addressed as its natural purposefulness becomes apparent in the schedule of the children's learning. While this approach emphasises the meaningful use of computers, one drawback is that of the logistical complications that would arise from the planning, resourcing and sequencing of a long-term plan. There is also the likelihood that some skills and techniques would be frequently repeated, while others could be neglected.

Reflection point

- *How will your computing lessons address the key features outlined here?*

The computing curriculum

Speaking at BETT in January 2012, Michael Gove MP, the Education Secretary at the time, described existing ICT in schools as 'harmful and dull' (*Telegraph* 2012), indicating that children needed to be aligned with the demands of a modern, technological workplace, in which they will enter the job market. His vision was for these children to be equipped with skills in coding and programming rather than the skills required to complete a spreadsheet.

The rhetoric here was clear. The curriculum reiterated this point in the outlined 'purpose of study', which indicated that children should work 'at a level suitable for the future workplace', describing the children as 'active participants in a digital world' (DfE 2013).

The essence of this may be perceived as being more relevant to those young adults working at Key Stage 3 rather than the young children working at Key Stage 2. However, the wording of the curriculum document highlights this shift in emphasis, as it requires Key Stage 1 children to 'understand what algorithms are', to 'create and debug simple programs' and to 'use logical reasoning'. For Key Stage 1 children and teachers, this may seem a little daunting and challenging, while it cannot be denied that the potential possibilities for outstanding, inspiring and creative work are endless. This is extended to Key Stage 2. Here, children are challenged to 'create a range of programs, systems and content that accomplish given goals' (DfE 2013). Is it too much to imagine that, in a few years' time, a lucrative Year 6 project could provide the funds for pupils to pay for their own university places?

Such advancements cost money and can raise concerns among staff. Some would argue that the pressures of being a teacher mean there is little time to learn new skills associated with such wholesale changes, even with the best will in the world. However, many practitioners, who can see past the logistical chaos created by the changes, recognise that, first, the changes are not as wholesale as was first imagined, and second, that the potential of the curriculum leaves schools with endless opportunities in creating their own bespoke curriculum, and enhancing the teaching and learning experiences for both teacher and child.

In the short time that the National Curriculum for ICT was dis-applied, some schools took the opportunity this freedom had presented them with and designed a new curriculum for their schools. In a school I work closely with, its Year 3 children were designing games in their computing lessons, a trend that was matched across the country. Creating a new curriculum, for many schools, has been a rewarding experience, which was validated upon the arrival of the published curriculum in 2013. It provided the opportunity to move away from less inspiring aspects of the more commonly found office-based tasks. Raspberry Pi projects have begun springing up in primary schools up and down the country, as have coding clubs. Children are working on Python scripts in order to write their own programs. This can be seen as the first step towards children writing code for any number of outcomes and the preparation required for their future place in the workforce, rather than spending all their time on the less creative uses of computers. However, this is not to say that 'office' skills are no longer valued. As indicated earlier, it is important to note that the skills required to word process, create a poster, use a spreadsheet and create a PowerPoint file have not been overlooked or devalued. These more traditional skills are recognised in the aims of the curriculum, which state that all pupils are 'responsible, competent, confident and creative users of information and communication technology'. This statement also alludes to the importance of e-safety with the inclusion of the word 'responsible'.

The content of the curriculum refers to the children's ability to 'select, use and combine a variety of software', and to 'search effectively and to consider how data is provided' (DfE 2013). Teachers familiar with older versions of the curriculum will be able to identify aspects of 'exchanging and sharing information' and 'finding things out' within this latest version.

The selection of words used in the curriculum document is interesting and open to interpretation. For instance, the use of the word 'collaboration' in the curriculum document could be interpreted as referring to cloud computing, with services such as Google Drive, making this an easily accessible feature to implement in school. However, of course, there is a more traditional interpretation whereby children work together in small teams towards problem solving and producing a shared end product.

Future proofing the curriculum is also evident in some of the words that are utilised in the document. The Aims of the Curriculum state that children 'can evaluate and apply information technology, including new or unfamiliar technologies'. The phrase 'new or unfamiliar technologies' would, at some point, describe the most mundane of technologies that we treat as commonplace today. Twelve years ago, an interactive whiteboard arriving in a classroom would have provoked a 'wooo' of excitement and appreciation from first-time users. Today, it is an expectation that a classroom would have such a device, and many schools are on their second or third version of such technology. More recently, schools have been investing in iPads and other tablets secure in the knowledge that, in two or three years' time, the hardware will need upgrading and replacing or will have been usurped completely by some 'new technology' that, sitting here, reading this, we are not yet aware of.

Reflection point

- *The computing curriculum allows you to develop interesting, challenging and relevant lessons. How will you embrace these opportunities to provide powerful teaching and learning experiences for your class?*

The pedagogy of computing

Computing capability is widely recognised as identifying the concepts, skills and techniques required to progress in computing. This is developed by Kennewell, Parkinson and Tanner (2000), and Simpson and Toyn (2012), and is advocated by a wide range of services and materials produced for schools, such as Herefordshire Council School Improvement Service (2008). It defines computing capability, stating that 'True ICT capability is attained when a child has knowledge and an understanding of the concepts involved, has acquired the necessary skills and can apply these to new learning situations.' They go on to emphasise that 'the extent to which they (the children) can do this independently and appropriately ... defines their level of capability' (Herefordshire Council 2008).

The challenge for schools is to best accommodate and serve a vibrant subject such as computing in their timetables. As discussed in an earlier section, this could well differ drastically from school to school and there could be any number of reasons for this, such as timetabling issues, staff subject knowledge and confidence, and issues around the resourcing of the subject as well as the available technical support.

Simpson and Toyn (2012) draw a nice analogy when describing how a tech user first comes to terms with a new gadget and finds her/himself in the throes of learning how to use it. Simpson and Toyn (2012) identify that initially motivation would have been high, as you knew what the device you were using was capable of, and the purpose for which you bought it provided the impetus for you to learn how to use it. This learning may have taken place in different ways. You may have opened the box and tried to figure it out for yourself, you may have been shown how to use it or you may have read the instructions. Despite your initial unfamiliarity with the device, you learned how to use the functions and to use the equipment for the purpose you bought it for. At first, you may have been more than aware of your use, you may have been cautious not to break it and anxious to get it right. You may have even referred back to the manual or asked to be shown again. Shortly, however, you grew confident in your ability to use the device until it became second nature. Think of this in terms of getting a new mobile phone or a new digital camera. The process is similar to learning to drive a car or ride a bike. You no longer think about each individual step, you just do it. Simpson and Toyn (2012) identify a further step whereby you become the teacher. Your skills and knowledge are to be shared and you soon find yourself demonstrating, modelling and discussing the features of your device with someone to whom these are less familiar. With this context, we can think clearly about how we might introduce a new piece of software or a new application to our class, remembering the fear of the unknown but also the sense of excitement that is created when we use something new for the first time.

Pedagogically, using technology can have a very different feel to it than the learning that takes place in other subjects. Many schools will be able to offer their children one-to-one provision with a computer in a computing suite or with a laptop or a tablet. This can have an incredible impact on the type of activity that the children engage with and the way in which they learn. For instance, some software programs will offer support as part of the way in which the program runs. This may be in the form of a help menu or a pop-up box or a prompt if you try to do something incorrectly, or a set of tutorials.

Such an approach may prove useful in aiding a child who has become stuck at a particular point, or in helping an able child in progressing. However, such intervention may not suit all learners and does not constitute teaching. What does such an approach say about the role of the teacher in the lesson? Prompts and help menus will not be enough to consolidate understanding and will merely serve to help the child over a hurdle in their development of their skills. Computing capability will not be developed, as purposeful learning experiences need to be managed, structured and meaningful. This will better ensure that a deep level of learning is taking place.

The ability to design such quality learning experiences stems from the subject knowledge and deep understanding of the teacher or trainee teacher. This links directly to the teacher standards and your own subject and curriculum knowledge, as well as an understanding of the needs of the individual children in your class and the opportunities you can provide for them.

It may be of concern to you as a conscientious practitioner, that the word 'skills' seems to be implicit in the teaching and learning that takes place in computing. This is only right, for computing is not solely concerned with the skills of using a piece of software. The understanding of how to use software is important, but so is the understanding of how the software works. The computing curriculum deals with the knowledge and understanding of how technology works. This is perhaps best highlighted in the computer science aspect of the curriculum that requires Key Stage 1 children to 'understand what algorithms are' and that 'programs execute by following precise and unambiguous instructions' (DfE 2013).

Kennewell (2000) recognises that a deep understanding of computing also includes an understanding of when and when not to use technology. The example given here is that of leaving a note for the milkman (although perhaps part of the lesson might be spent establishing what a milkman was!). This example considers the time and effort involved in booting up the computer, typing out your note for the milkman, printing it off and putting it outside. The argument is that, for this task, a simple handwritten note would suffice. Whereas, if you were applying for a job or writing a letter of complaint, then the task would be better served by the use of technology in order to create a better impression and afford you the luxury of key features, such as provisionality. Knowing when and when not to use technology is an important aspect of developing an understanding of computing capability.

Another consideration, while thinking about the pedagogy of computing, is how the lessons themselves are organised. We have already considered how the wealth of resources may impact upon the types of lesson we teach and design, and how the way in which the school has chosen to organise the hardware available will impact on lessons across the school. However, another consideration occurs at the planning stage and is undertaken by each individual teacher. For certain activities, the class teacher may well decide that the children would learn more effectively by working in pairs or trios rather than individually. This instantly provides the opportunity for dialogic talk and collaborative work between the learners. This provides the opportunity for the children to nudge one another towards developing their learning and, through discussion, establishing new boundaries to their collective knowledge and understanding. This is often the case in lessons, when children share their thoughts and understanding, and help one another to progress further.

Such learning experiences, which are designed to incorporate collegiate learning and collaborative work, also provide opportunities for the teacher to discuss progress with each child, allowing them to explain how they worked something out, and providing the opportunity for the teacher to check knowledge, understanding and pupil progress. This aspect of the teacher's role in the learning process is easy to overlook, but it is an essential aspect to the learning that takes place. As we discovered earlier, some software programs provide guidance and support within the program itself, others provide assessment opportunities, scoring systems, tracking and feedback on various activities; however, while these aspects of each program may be seen as advantageous in many ways, they do not replace the expertise of the practitioner or the bespoke intervention via which a thorough and conscientious teacher would enhance each learning experience by contributing timely teaching points, querying decisions and otherwise providing opportunities for the children to explain their work, decision making and thoughts at each stage of the lesson. This contribution can never be replaced or underestimated.

Reflection point

- *How will you ensure that your computing lessons develop understanding as well as skills?*

The computing teacher's toolkit

Providing a toolkit of practical activities and lesson ideas for computing comes with the proviso that it is understood that each given activity is taken from part of a scheme of work or progression of activities, and that they are not intended as standalone activities as they appear on the page here. Rather, it is anticipated that the reader will take on board the ideas presented here and adapt them to the needs of their own class. In each case, I have matched the activity to the relevant section of the 2014 computing curriculum, although each task can be simplified or extended to suit your own purposes.

Humpty had a great fall

Key Stage 1 – use technology purposefully to create, organise, store, manipulate and retrieve digital content.

This activity is derived from the original QCA schemes of work and is designed to provide a purpose for the children to use the functions of a word processor. It introduces some tools and consolidates use of others. In a shared folder on the school drive, children open a document that you have prepared, labelled 'Humpty'. Once opened on the screen, the children will be presented with the well-known nursery rhyme with each line jumbled up, for example...

All the King's horses and all the King's men
Humpty Dumpty sat on a wall
Couldn't put Humpty together again
Humpty Dumpty had a great fall

The task is for the children to rearrange the lines of the rhyme into the correct order by using the 'cut' and 'paste' features of a word-processing package. This requires the children to control the mouse or track pad, and to highlight text in order to complete the task efficiently and effectively. Of course, at the discretion of the teacher, the text can be altered in order to suit the texts and topics the class are studying in other subjects. Alternatively, the same task can simply use other texts, such as the reordering of the obstacles that the family face in 'We're going on a bear hunt' (Rosen and Oxenbury 1993) or reordering the food that the hungry caterpillar eats (Carle 2002).

Slalom run

Key Stage 1 – understand what algorithms are, how they are implemented as programs on digital devices, and that programs execute by following precise and unambiguous instructions.

When introducing a floor turtle at Key Stage 1, a context for the work can be provided through use of a story, or reason as to why the floor turtle needs to be moved. The children might be challenged to program their turtle to complete a route, drive through a goal, or move through and round skittles in order to complete a slalom run. These tasks can be developed in several ways. First, the children can be challenged to program their floor turtle to visit various points around the room. Each point may contain a fact or a symbol or clue as to the next point to visit, in this way creating a treasure hunt around the room. In establishing a correct sequence the need for an organised and correct response from the children in programming their floor turtle is evident, as is the 'fun' of the activity. Teachers may like to take the 'We're going on a bear hunt' idea from the previous activity and challenge the children to visit each location in sequence, just as the family do in the book. The course is set by the teacher and therefore can be as complicated or as easy as best suits the needs of the class.

In order to add another dimension to such tasks, and further explore aspects of the curriculum, the children can be presented with a set of cards. Each card contains a route (algorithm) and the children are challenged to predict which of the cards is correct, or would provide the fastest route, or is hopelessly off-course. This requires the children to predict, solve problems and use their logical reasoning skills.

Radio radio

Key Stage 2 – select, use and combine a variety of software on a range of digital devices to design and create a range of programs, systems and content that accomplish given goals, including presenting data and information.

Technology is ever changing and, with each new advancement, possibilities and opportunities begin to present themselves. A school I visited recently had its own recording studio, which acted as a radio station at lunchtimes. Creating content for a school radio station could take the form of the children producing podcasts and audio files as part of their work in other subject areas. Whereas in the past the children might have been challenged to create a poster or a PowerPoint file, the children here can be tasked with demonstrating their knowledge and understanding of, let's say, history, in the form of a radio show or a documentary. This provides opportunities for English work as well as the obvious strong links with the topic or theme that is the inspiration for the computing work. While some schools do have the facility to broadcast the children's work, others might share the audio files or podcasts via QR codes or a link on the school website. Work can easily be shared with parents as well as other classes in school, generating pride and a real sense of achievement among the children.

Scratch it!

Key Stage 2 – design, write and debug programs that accomplish specific goals; use sequence, selection and repetition in programs; use logical reasoning to explain how some simple algorithms work, and to detect and correct errors in algorithms and programs.

Scratch is a free resource that can be accessed via the MITT website; once you have an account, you can create all sorts of algorithms and processes in order to create games and other applications. This is all done through the use of code blocks. Other systems do exist, such as Kodu, and – as with other resources – the decision as to which system to use will vary across the country from school to school.

Simple tasks offer a great way to introduce applications to the children. Creating a chase game, or a version of a classic like 'pong' or 'breakout', will provide a sense of achievement (for you and the children). However, you will want your children to create the coding for their very own masterpieces; these may include joke telling, whereby characters on the screen tell each other a joke, mazes, quick response games and quizzes. The beauty of 'Scratch' is that you can create pretty much anything you can think of, making it the ideal partner for many cross-curricular topics as well as an ideal application for the delivery of the computer science aspects of the computing curriculum.

For instance, I have written elsewhere about the possibility of creating a quiz based upon a history topic the children are studying. While this would be a more than suitable task to address the computer science aspects of the National Curriculum, it can be further enhanced by challenging the children to create tutorial cards to help other children to create the aforementioned quiz. In this way, the children not only demonstrate their skills and abilities to create the game, but also their knowledge and understanding in order to explain and communicate to someone else how to make the game.

Stop it!

Key Stage 2 – select, use and combine a variety of software on a range of digital devices to design and create a range of programs, systems and content that accomplish given goals, including presenting data and information.

Everybody wants to be in the movies, right? Well, here is your chance. All you need is a stop-frame animation software package, a camera and some Lego.

As with earlier suggested activities, this one can also be adapted to suit your curriculum topics and the needs of the children in your class. I have seen this activity completed successfully with traditional fairy tales as the theme. However, I have also delivered the same sessions with e-safety messages as the focus. In this case, this activity would also address the e-safety aspects of the computing curriculum, which requires children to 'use technology safely, respectfully and responsibly; recognise acceptable/unacceptable behaviour; identify a range of ways to report concerns about content and contact' (DfE 2013).

In groups – as collaborative learning is often best for such projects – the children are given a particular e-safety concern, such as what to do if an inappropriate image appears on the screen, keeping your personal information private or cyber bullying. The children then script a short scene, designed to raise awareness of their given e-safety area, and provide guidance as to what to do if it happens to you. With the use of Lego characters (of course, other options are available such as building your own plasticine people) the children create their stop-frame animation movie, which, as with other pieces of work, can be shared with other classes in a variety of ways in order to raise awareness and spread the e-safety message.

Summary of key points

This chapter has looked at the position of computing in the primary school. We have investigated how computing has changed radically over the years, and have also considered why the delivery of computing varies from school to school and the reasons for this. We have also explored the language used in the 2014 curriculum, and how computer science can be adopted within our schools. We have explored the identity of computing as a subject and the ways in which skills, knowledge and understanding are developed within the subject through ideas such as the key features of computing and computing capability.

In this chapter we have:

- explored the position of computing in the primary school
- investigated how computing has changed radically over the years
- considered why the delivery of computing varies from school to school, and the reasons for this
- explored the language used in the 2014 curriculum, and how computer science can be adopted within our schools
- recognised the identity of computing as a subject, and the ways in which skills, knowledge and understanding are developed within the subject through ideas such as the key features of ICT and ICT capability.

The purpose of this chapter is to provide a useful springboard for you to develop your own ideas for your own considered, inspiring and thoughtful computing lessons. After all, that must be the main aim of every teacher.

References

Allen, J., Potter, J., Sharp, J. and Turvey, K. (2012) *Primary ICT: Knowledge, Understanding and Practice*, 5th edn. Exeter: Learning Matters.

Carle, E. (2002) *The Very Hungry Caterpillar*. London: Puffin.

Department for Education (DfE) (2013) *The National Curriculum for England Framework Document*. London: DfE.

Kennewell, S., Parkinson, J. and Tanner, H. (2000) *Developing the ICT Capable School*. London: Routledge.

Ofsted (2014) *Information and Communication Technology (ICT) Survey Visits*. London: Ofsted.

Rosen, M. and Oxenbury, H. (1993) *We're Going on a Bear Hunt*. London: Walker Books.

Simpson, D. and Toyn, M (2012) *Primary ICT Across the Curriculum*, 2nd edn. Exeter: Learning Matters.

Online sources

Herefordshire Council School Improvement Service (2008) www.herefordshire.gov.uk/education-and-learning/schools/school-management/school-improvement (accessed August 2014)

Kodu (2014) www.kodugamelab.com/ (accessed August 2014)

Lego (2014) www.lego.com/en-gb (accessed August 2014)

MITT (2014) http://scratch.mit.edu/ (accessed August 2014)

Python (2014) www.python.org (accessed August 2014)

Raspberry Pi (2014) www.raspberrypi.org (accessed August 2014)

Telegraph (2012) www.telegraph.co.uk/technology/9007467/Dull-technology-school-lessons-to-be-replaced.html (accessed August 2014)

4 Design & technology

Wendy Dixon

Have you ever walked into a primary classroom and noticed unfinished, unvalued design & technology projects? Quite often these projects are either on the side, on the floor or in the corner waiting for their final destination: the bin. In addition to this, craft lessons are often mistaken for design & technology projects, with children going home with identical completed items. It is easy for practitioners to often shy away from technical skills due to a lack of subject knowledge, which can diminish confidence when, quite easily, both of these scenarios could so easily be avoided. A little more understanding of the subject, a little more enthusiasm and much more fun can change the dimension of a design & technology unit of work. However, this can be a little daunting at the start of your teaching career, especially when a teacher must demonstrate good subject and curriculum knowledge, which when given the range of subjects that a primary teacher needs to be able to implement can be considered no mean feat.

This chapter explores the three-lens lens model in relation to design & technology, and considers the identity of this sometimes misunderstood aspect of the curriculum. If taught well children will identify design & technology as one of their favourite subjects, because they find that making decisions, creating new and original items, and having freedom to investigate is really appealing (DATA 2014). To achieve this yourself you will find here ideas on how to plan alongside pedagogy with a selection of toolkit ideas that are designed to inspire you as well as the children, hopefully dispelling any poor past experiences that may have affected your attitude to this subject.

The identity of design & technology

We all have memories of making things in school; this could be an Easter basket at primary school, or food technology, wood or metal work at high school. Even before that someone will probably have allowed you to make things, and you will have developed skills that will have complemented your engagement with design & technology, such as painting, drawing, cutting out or mixing food ingredients. But were the projects (the items you made) true to the definition of a design & technology project, or were they craft items? Were your projects different to others or were they all the same? Let us consider in more depth what the identity of design & technology is believed to be.

From Ofsted's perspective, design & technology has three elements:

1. designing and making a product, with...
2. a given audience, and with...
3. a purpose.

This, Ofsted believes, will enable children to generate ideas that will solve a given problem. Problem solving – a creative thinking skill – has been highlighted in design & technology for a long time now and there has been much debate as to whether this skill can be transferred to problem solving in other subjects (for example, mathematics) or vice versa. Although the nature of a project you may give to the children does not seem to present itself as solving a problem (e.g. create a filling for a sandwich) this skill is still nevertheless vital to the process of its creation (Wilson 2011).

Contemporary thoughts – such as those of Sir James Dyson, a modern-day inventor, famous for his vacuum technology – reveal a little more about this subject's identity. Dyson said that he believed 'design & technology is about making things work that people want and that work well. Creating these things is hugely exciting: it is an inventive, fun activity.'

Design & technology allows the perfection of ideas through its process. The development of the bike illustrates the nature of design & technology very well. The very first bike did not have brakes or moving handlebars; it did not have pneumatic tyres and it did not have a light metal frame. All of these things have been developed over time to solve the problems that will have occurred within the original design.

The acknowledgement of inventors and inventions should be embedded in the curriculum as citizenship is a strong component of design & technology, which allows children to make links with industry and the world of work. The concept of manufacturing and becoming responsible for the use of resources is addressed practically, and the effects that new technologies have on society are explored. Interwoven throughout is the recognition of the implications all of this can have for people and places. Who invents and why they invent can offer children an insight into our ever changing world. Therefore it is important that children understand the role of designers within society. They should be informed of how key events and individuals have helped shape the world they live in.

One example of this is Norwegian office manager Johann Vaaler, who in 1899 found that he had a problem: he was unable to organise a pile of papers. Through trial and error Vaaler found a solution – the wire paper clip. A more recent example is that of Fiona Fairhurst who, in 2004, invented Fastskin swimwear. She was inspired by the overlapping scales of shark skin and, through her idea, this invention has helped swimmers travel faster through water. Her invention has been so successful that it has been banned from some swimming competitions as it was seen to put those swimmers who were not wearing the swimwear at a disadvantage! Children can also relate to the zip fastener as they probably use one every day, but have they thought about who invented it and where the idea came from? Gideon Sundback invented the zip fastener in 1913, but he worked on other ideas of hook-and-eye fastenings before finally perfecting the zip we have today.

In addition to citizenship, when children are engaging with a design & technology project there is potential for moral, spiritual and social development. This is encouraged through positive engagement, while taking into account the preferences of others, sharing and cooperating and learning to respect others' contributions, their culture and their values. The identity of design & technology has a character that is determined by its community of experts, and the practice of those experts influences pedagogy and encourages real creativity (Davies 2004; Ewens 2014). With all this in mind, design & technology projects should be original, have value and should solve a problem.

To find out more about the identity of design & technology a useful document is Ofsted's most recent subject-specific survey of primary design & technology, *Meeting Technical Challenges* (published March 2011). The evidence gathered from inspections was collated to provide an Ofsted training document in order to support the delivery and enhancement of this subject (Ofsted 2012).

Reflection points

- *List the projects you can remember completing at school, and consider whether they were design & technology or craft projects.*
- *Look at the Ofsted training document,* Meeting Technical Challenges, *and list the projects that you think are original and of value.*

The design & technology curriculum

Endorsed by the Design & Technology Association (DATA) the purpose of design & technology, as defined by the National Curriculum, is that it should be inspiring, rigorous and practical, while developing a sense of belonging in the society (and beyond) in which the children live.

Before the introduction of a National Curriculum, design & technology was identified in the primary timetable as craft or needlework lessons. In 1988 the first Working Group for Science included in its remit design & technology, with this later becoming independent of science and more formally structured. The curriculum today has its main theme focusing on the acquisition of skills, with the belief that it will allow children to become fully equipped citizens for the future. This comes close to the reforms that were outlined in the Ruskin Speech (1976) by James Callaghan (Ewens 2014), and also reflects the long-held view that design & technology should raise technological competence and awareness in children.

As part of the National Curriculum, design & technology is compulsory and has statutory programmes of study for primary schools in both Key Stage 1 and Key Stage 2. However, it is important to note here that the increase and diversification of schools in the English school system has allowed academies and free schools to define their own curricula (Ewens 2014). Therefore, it is important to be open to this variance and expect that, in maintained schools, as long as the National Curriculum is taught the schools are free to choose how they organise their school day.

Curriculum aims

The use of subject knowledge and key skills from other areas of the curriculum are stressed in the curriculum, allowing you extensive opportunities for cross-curricular and thematic teaching.

Subject content

The National Curriculum offers example content for design & technology, but this is very limited to allow teachers freedom to explore pedagogy and toolkit. In Key Stage 1, practical activities within a range of relevant contexts are outlined with an emphasis that projects should be purposeful, functional and appealing, and based on a process of design, make and evaluate. The Key Stage 2 curriculum builds on this by offering continuity and progression for children from Key Stage 1, directing you to work within a range of relevant contexts following the same design, make and evaluate process. You will see that, in Key Stage 2, you are asked to expand children's technical knowledge while developing research skills; this includes the use of new technologies to inform their projects, and increases the range of tools and equipment. The emphasis in both key stages on instilling a love of cooking, and being able to apply the principles of nutrition and healthy eating adds another exciting dimension to the programme of study. This major change has given design & technology two strands: design and making, and cooking and nutrition.

Technical knowledge

In recent years there has been a clear focus on the development of children's technical vocabulary in all aspects of the curriculum. In design & technology there are many opportunities to develop a specialist vocabulary. This can be done through children engaging with projects where they are introduced to using tools, equipment and materials, and encouraged to examine and employ them through their reading and writing. The range of technical knowledge for children to explore is quite minimal in its outline in the National Curriculum, but this offers extensive opportunities for you to encourage children to investigate and engage with new skills. Remember that these skills need to be fully understood and mastered by you as the teacher before embarking on a project.

Food

In Key Stage 1 children are expected to know where food comes from, while in Key Stage 2 children's knowledge should extend to seasonality and how a range of ingredients are grown, reared, caught and processed.

Attainment targets

Attainment targets are short but are concerned with the full content of the programme of study. Continuity and progression through the primary school's phases will be shown in the scheme of work. This relates to the programmes of study, and ensures that children's skills are developed and applied in units of work (DfE 2013).

Long-term planning

In order to ensure that all the National Curriculum requirements are met, and that continuity and progression are secured, a long-term plan can offer a good overview of the school design & technology curriculum. This plan then feeds the medium-term plan or a unit of work (an example of such is described later in this chapter).

Health and safety, and hygiene

In the National Curriculum children are expected to use a wide range of tools and equipment to cut, shape, join and finish. All aspects of health and safety should be explored and addressed so that children can do this safely within your classroom. To receive a burn from a hot-glue gun can be extremely painful, but children in Key Stage 2 should be encouraged to use them, safely. An explanation at the start of the lesson on their use, and perhaps initially adult support, will be productive in the safe use of glue guns. A poster that outlines correct usage of all tools and equipment is useful so that you can refer to it during lessons; it also acts as a good reminder when children are working independently. To ensure full ownership of the health and safety and hygiene rules in your classroom make sure you involve the children in their development. In addition to your consideration of the safe use of equipment, schools will also encourage risk assessments as part of the design & technology curriculum; these are usually led by the subject coordinator.

When you are working with food, hygiene is extremely important. Children should be made fully aware of how and why food hygiene is necessary. They should also know that:

- food needs to be handled in a clean environment
- water should be available for clearing up

- the sink should not be used for clay or paint
- food in a fridge should be labelled with a date
- equipment should be kept separate for food work, and
- children should be aware of how to prepare themselves to work with food.

Reflection points

- *Have a look at the DATA website and download the long-term plan example.*
- *What methods will you use to empower children in their engagement of health and safety, and hygiene?*

The pedagogy of design & technology

A full appreciation and understanding of design & technology and the skills to be taught will enable you to inspire children with a sense of audience and purpose. This will help you to give children an opportunity to develop a sense of place in the past, present and future. Research has shown that teaching them design will enhance their ability to learn, respond creatively to challenges and actively participate in society's evolution (Miller 2011). However, it may be that you are quite secure in your subject knowledge but perhaps need to know this subject in a way that allows you to teach it effectively.

Quite clearly it is recognised that design & technology is a hands-on part of the curriculum in which you should be encouraging children to make real and tangible projects. You can discuss designs and look at projects made by others, but children will learn more through a hands-on approach, which allows them to touch, to explore, to engage, to think and to experiment (you may want to consider here the Cone of Learning developed by Edgar Dale). Before implementing a project with children, have a think about having a go yourself. Apart from making you familiar with the skills the children will need, this can be useful in the recognition of pitfalls that the children may come across.

Before embarking on any project you need to ensure that the classroom is a safe and secure environment where 'having a go' is valued and perceived failure is seen as part of a process on the road to success. Research by the Hay/McBer Group (2000) has suggested that the environment a teacher creates in his or her classroom contributes to whether teaching is effective or not. You must recognise that the fear of failure can seriously inhibit a child's engagement with a design & technology project, and the impact of this will therefore most likely inhibit outcomes. Outcomes from a design & technology project should be original and, for you to ensure that the children come up with something original, you need to prepare them to be wrong (Ken Robinson, NACCE Report 1999). Many successful designers refuse to acknowledge failure: Thomas Edison, a prolific inventor, did not feel that he had ever failed, just that he had discovered many other ways that would not work and that these forced him down a different path to a better place. When discussing designers and failure, children will probably initially relate better to those designers they already know. For example, Sir James Dyson admits that he fails constantly but that he learns from those mistakes.

Once you have secured a safe environment it is important for you to understand that in the teaching and planning of design & technology this subject is taught as a unit rather than a standalone lesson. Very often children are expected to complete projects without the necessary skills and in a limited amount of time. Schools often have set projects, and these should be planned in either half- or whole-term units to allow children to complete their project. However, not all schools have planned units of work prepared and an element of autonomy may be required in the delivery of this subject in both cases.

A design & technology unit can be taught entirely on its own but is very often taught within a theme and generally with cross-curricular links where children are allowed to use ideas from other areas of the curriculum. Try to make the context motivating so that children can discover aspects of other parts of the curriculum (DATA 2014). Ultimately your aim will be to secure high standards through high-quality subject teaching applied through cross-curricular projects. The Rose Report (2009) identified that, if essential knowledge and skills are learned through high-quality subject teaching, with opportunities for this knowledge to be applied in cross-curricular studies, then high standards will be secured. Make sure that any cross-curricular links you make are explicit and meaningful so that children are able to recognise the distinctive nature of each subject. Take care to link subjects only where there is a meaningful overlap of knowledge, skills and/ or process.

It is important to nurture children so that they see challenges as the opportunity to be creative in mastering key skills and knowledge (Ewens 2014). We are fortunate that, over the years, education policy has enhanced positive opportunities for embedding creativity in the curriculum, and this has been significantly developed since it was highlighted in the Roberts Report (2006). The Rose Report (Rose 2009), too, emphasises the need for a broad and balanced entitlement, encouraging creativity and allowing children to become life-long learners, making connections between previously unconnected ideas (Koestler 1964) with Dyson's famous example of a tornado and the Dyson vacuum cleaner.

How to plan a design & technology unit of work

When thinking about planning it is important to note that, for children, having to think about specific purposes and users for their products is much more demanding than simply following instructions to make something. Therefore your unit of work should encourage children to think, decide and plan, as well as go and create; this can make the results as rewarding for you as they are for them (DATA 2014).

The planning and delivery of this subject within this chapter uses a five-stage process that addresses the three elements identified by Ofsted: designed and made product, audience (Who is it for?) and purpose (Why are you making it?).

These five stages are:

1. Product Analysis
2. Design

3. Key Skills
4. Make
5. Evaluate.

These five stages address the project but to achieve audience and purpose it is important to place this process within a meaningful context. Therefore as you open your unit of work, children need to be immersed in the work and wonders of designers, both from the past and the present. This should then be followed by an appropriate and engaging stimulus carefully chosen to place the project in a meaningful context.

Reflection points

- *Think about how skills learned in other subjects can be used in design & technology.*
- *In your observations of other practitioners, consider the strategies they have in place to secure a safe and motivating classroom environment.*

The design & technology teacher's toolkit

The design & technology teacher's toolkit is a collection of ideas that can be developed or adapted to the context in which they are set, and designed to suit different year groups/ key stages. Two completed units of work are offered as examples for you to use or adapt.

Themes

Decide whether you are working within a theme or not. A theme is generally agreed from either a whole school or key stage approach, but will always open up many opportunities for you to be creative in your planning.

Key skills

Once you have identified your theme it is important to think of the key skills that you would like to include in your project (see Table 4.1). This decision can be informed from a variety of sources, such as children's prior engagement with design & technology or other topics in other areas of the curriculum. The project you choose will rely on the skills that you identify.

Deciding on your project

Once you have identified the key skills that will work within your theme or subject focus, you need to decide on a project. In this project children need to be able to create and imagine something that does not already exist (Wilson 2011).

Table 4.1 D&T key skills

Key Stage 1			
Food	**Textiles**	**Construction**	**Sheet materials**
• **cut, peel, grate, chop** • work safely and hygienically • **measure and weigh using non-statutory measures, e.g. spoons, cups**	• **colour fabrics using, e.g., fabric paints, printing, painting** • join fabrics using running stitch, glue, staples, tape • **decorate fabrics with buttons, beads, sequins, ribbon**	• **make vehicles with free-running wheels** • create wheels and axles using dowel, cotton reels, tubes • **attach wheels using an axle** • join different materials, e.g. glue, tape • **use a template** • cut dowel using hacksaw and bench hook	• **fold, tear and cut paper and card** • roll paper to create tubes • **cut along lines, straight and curved** • curl paper • **use hole punch** • use paper fasteners for card linkages • **investigate how to strengthen sheet materials** • investigate joinings
Lower Key Stage 2			
Food	**Textiles**	**Construction**	**Sheet materials**
• **follow instructions** • join and combine a range of ingredients • **work safely and hygienically** • measure and weigh ingredients	• **understand seam allowance** • join fabrics using running stitch, over sewing and back stitch • **explore fastenings** • create a simple pattern	• **incorporate a circuit with a bulb** • create shell or frame structures • **measure to 1 cm** • use a glue gun	• **cut slots** • cut internal shapes • **use lolly sticks to make levers and linkages** • explore pop-ups • **create nets**
Upper Key Stage 2			
Food	**Textiles**	**Construction**	**Sheet materials**
• **select and prepare foods for a purpose** • weigh and measure using scales • **cut and shape ingredients, e.g. grating** • work safely and hygienically	• **create 3D products** • understand pattern layout • **pin and tack fabric** • use over sewing, back stitch, blanket stitch or machine stitching to join fabric	• **use a bradawl** • use hand drill • **cut wood, dowel to 1 mm** • join materials • **use a motor and switch** • use ICT to control • **use a glue gun**	• **cut slots** • cut accurately • **join and combine materials** • use craft knife

Making links with designers, inventors and inventions

Children enjoy the story behind everyday objects, and to know the how, when and why things were invented gives a purpose to their learning.

Putting learning into a meaningful context

A meaningful context can be established by ensuring that the children are familiar with the theme in which you are placing the project. The use of music, props, and so on, is effective in the creation of an atmosphere, and an effective stimulus can introduce the project and place it within this context quickly.

Choosing a stimulus

Ideas for such will be explored later in the chapter.

Creating a design scenario

A design scenario is similar to telling a story. It places the children further into the context and can be used to further develop a sense of audience and purpose for the project.

Summarising the project with a design brief

A detailed outline of the overall objectives for the project can be detailed within a design brief ensuring that specific guidelines are given and boundaries are created.

Once you have completed all of these stages you will be ready to begin the five-stage process.

Stage one: product analysis

The project that has been decided upon will dictate the nature of the product analysis. You may wish to invite a speaker, go on a school visit and/or you may ask the children to take things apart to investigate how they work. Whatever you decide should immerse the children in the project. (It is important to note here that any school visit or trip must be risk assessed and approved through the school's educational visit coordinator.)

Stage two: design

All stages are important, but this stage is often rushed and sometimes 'missed' as the value of it is not recognised by teachers or children. Using their knowledge from the product analysis stage, you should encourage the children to use brainstorming or blue-sky thinking in the early stages of their design. Once you and the children feel that the design is ready to work with, the next step is to identify the key skills they will need in order to complete their project.

Stage three: key skills

With careful consideration of their designs children will discuss what key skills they need. The need to support this discussion will depend on the age of the children you are teaching.

The success of engaging with any project will depend on some of the skills to be used, such as cutting. The use of focused practical tasks can then be given, which can allow for some very specific teaching of technique and process (Wilton 2014). These tasks, or the practice of skills (such as cutting), do not necessarily need to be within the design & technology unit, but could be developed through a cross-curricular approach to create skills that are 'knowledge in context' (Bennett 2014).

Stage four: make
During the 'making' stage children should be encouraged to use their design but they should understand that they have the freedom to make alterations if necessary to their project – at the same time noting what they changed and why.

Stage five: evaluate
The creative methods that can be used (see ideas in toolkit) to assess learning should complement the nature of the unit of work. The intentions behind assessment are many and varied, and with design & technology it is important to develop the ability in children to self-assess and peer assess (Wilson 2011; Ewens 2014). These assessments are then taken to inform the next project.

Health and safety, and hygiene

As identified earlier, the importance of this aspect should be emphasised through clear instructions at the beginning of each lesson; this will embed health and safety into the ethos of your teaching.

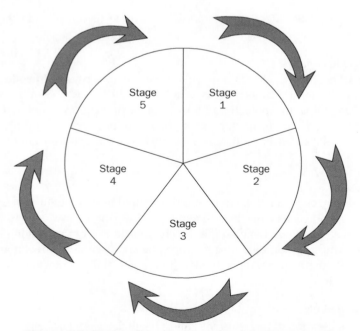

Figure 4.1 Design & technology planning process cycle

Suggested units of work

Idea one: celebrity kitchen

Table 4.2 Celebrity kitchen

Design & technology medium-term plan — 1 × two-week unit of work Key Stage 2
Project: Celebrity kitchen *(Enterprise Unit)*
Theme: Ourselves and others
Key skills: • incorporate a circuit with a bulb, buzzer • join different materials • measure to 1 cm/1 mm • use a glue gun • create nets • cut wood
Key vocabulary: inventors, inventions, scenario, design brief, invest, famous, analysis, mood board (see Figure 4.2)
Resources: YouTube clip, Millionaire quiz, envelopes with celebrities, price list of materials
Groupings: children to work in small groups of 4 or 5
Cross-curricular links: geography – *developing knowledge of the world;* mathematics – *measures, nets;* science – *creating a circuit;* history – *pupils should be taught about the lives of significant individuals in the past*

Lesson one: *Creating a meaningful context*	**Stimulus:** show children a YouTube clip of *Dragons' Den* or engage children with 'dragons' through role play using local businessmen/women. Children can discuss what it would be like to be a dragon – what businesses would they invest in? *Children to understand the role of 'dragons'*
Lesson two: subject identity *Designers/inventors/inventions*	**Inventions/inventors:** importance of inventors and inventions, discussion of impact on our lives of inventions. Choose inventions that would be appropriate. An invention that has made people wealthy; an invention that would be considered by one of the dragons, e.g. electric guitar made George Beauchamp a millionaire, patented in 1937; instant noodles launched in 1958, invented by Momofuku Ando; Sir Tim Berners-Lee, inventor of the World Wide Web. Use *Who Wants to be a Millionaire?* template to create a quiz with famous inventions/inventors for the children to choose through multiple choice

(Continued)

Table 4.2   Celebrity kitchen *(Continued)*

Lesson three: design scenario, design brief, outline of project process *Design specification:* Kitchen: *must reflect personality and character of chosen celebrity and must incorporate the use of at least one electric circuit* Create: *mood board and to-scale model* Costings: *to know how much the kitchen has cost (including labour)*	Show the **stimulus** again to remind the children of the context in which the project is set. **Design scenario:** tell the children that they have applied in groups to go into the Dragons' Den. They have to convince the dragons to invest in their business. Their business is to design tailor-made kitchens for celebrities; a kitchen of a celebrity's dreams. **Design brief:** ask the children to choose an envelope to reveal the name of a celebrity; the children will design a kitchen for this celebrity. The children are asked to provide a mood board and a scale model of the kitchen, complete with costings to present to the dragons. **Process:** tell the children the five-stage process that they will be going through in order to engage with this project
Lesson four/five: product analysis:	Questions to consider **Kitchen:** • How are kitchens designed? • How are things stored in a kitchen? • What kitchen appliances do I need? • What is the kitchen work triangle? • How much do kitchens cost? **Celebrity:** • Who is my celebrity? • What is my celebrity famous for? • What colours would they be associated with? • Can I think of any items that would identify that character? • What sort of personality do they have? **General:** • What will be their budget? • Where would I put an electric circuit? **Activity suggestions:** • Visit a kitchen showroom • Invite a kitchen designer in • Invite a 'celebrity' to outline what they would like in their kitchen • Research websites • Look at catalogues • Look at costings (you will probably provide this for the materials they will use) • Look at magazines

Table 4.2 Celebrity kitchen *(Continued)*

Lesson five/six: design	**Mood board:** the children need to gather the evidence they have collected from their research so that they can create a mood board for the celebrity they have been given (see example). The mood board will inform the kitchen design. **Kitchen:** using their mood board children will begin to design a scale model for their kitchen. They will need to consider the number of kitchen cupboards – base cabinets, wall cabinets – the type of worktops, the way in which the design will incorporate the kitchen work triangle; the consideration of an island and where the **electrics** will go. This can be scaffolded by the use of a grid depending on the support required for the age group you are teaching. There is also an opportunity here to include the use of technology in the design of the celebrity's kitchen. A kitchen design website may be used that has an interactive design. If preferred, apps can be used. Once they have decided on their design, children need to decide what **materials** they are going to use and list them, identifying the **cost** (you may wish to give them a budget to work with). The completed design should have instructions and labelled diagrams, complete mood board and list of resources required
Lesson seven/eight: key skills	**Identification of key skills:** in this lesson children are given the opportunity to reflect, share and discuss their designs. From this, collectively, the class will list the key skills they need to complete their project. Children should then be asked to assess their ability in each skill and plans then formulated to address these (these can be addressed in other areas of the curriculum)
Lesson eight/nine/ten: make	**Health and safety:** before allowing the children to begin making their project, a health and safety talk is required, with visual reminders displayed on the walls. **Make:** children use the time allocated to create their celebrity kitchen. They need to have time to build it, place a circuit in it, prepare a presentation for the dragons, including how much the kitchen cost, the money required from the dragons and the percentage of their business that they are happy to part with. If children want to make changes moving away from their design, ask them to note down any change and why they made it.

(Continued)

Table 4.2 Celebrity kitchen *(Continued)*

Lesson eleven/twelve: evaluation	**Presentation for dragons:** ensure the children are prepared to meet the dragons – play the YouTube video again or adults to role play each dragon. You may wish to create an environment to fit with the theme. The children will be asked to present their kitchens in whatever way they would like to. The dragons evaluate and decide whether they are going to invest, giving or not giving reasons for any decision they make. (It may be useful to show at some point the YouTube clip of a project that would not work – egg cooker – but a dragon still invested)

Figure 4.2 Example of a mood board

Idea two: The Lighthouse Keeper's Lunch (Armitage and Armitage 1994)

Table 4.3   Design a lunch for the lighthouse keeper

Design & technology medium-term plan — 1 × two-week unit of work Key Stage 1 or 2

Project: Design a lunch for the lighthouse keeper

Theme: Ourselves and others

Key skills:

Key Stage 1
- cut, peel, grate, chop
- work safely and hygienically
- measure and weigh using non-statutory measures, e.g. spoons, cups

Key Stage 2
- join and combine a range of ingredients
- work safely and hygienically
- measure and weigh ingredients

Key vocabulary: ingredients, lunch, safely, hygiene, measure

Resources: a variety of ingredients, cutlery and crockery

Groupings: children to work in pairs or small groups

Cross-curricular links: science, PSHE, literacy, geography

Lesson one: *Creating a meaningful context*	**Stimulus:** read the story of 'The Lighthouse Keeper's Lunch'. Role play the lighthouse keeper so that the children get a flavour of what it is like to be one
Lesson two: subject identity *Designers/inventors/inventions*	**Inventions/Inventors:** there are lots of food-related inventions, but the children may be interested in the invention of fizzy drinks, chocolate, etc.
Lesson three: design scenario, design brief, outline of project process *Design specification*	Read the book again. **Design scenario:** tell the children that the lighthouse keeper would like a new lunch and that he would like them to create some sandwiches that he could choose from. When they have designed them, he will taste them and say yes or no. **Design brief:** children are to design a filling for a sandwich that would suit the lighthouse keeper. They are able to choose the type of bread the sandwich will be made in. **Process:** tell the children the five-stage process that they will be going through in order to engage with this project

(Continued)

Table 4.3 Design a lunch for the lighthouse keeper *(Continued)*

Lesson four/five: product analysis	Questions to consider
	Lighthouse keeper • What foods does the housekeeper like? • What does his wife like making? • What kind of bread does he like? • Does he have a fridge? • How much does he like to eat? • How much does he want to spend? **Ingredients** • What is a recipe? • What are healthy ingredients? • What foods go together? • What sandwiches do supermarkets provide? • What types of bread are there? **Activity suggestions:** • Invite the lighthouse keeper and his wife to be interviewed by the children (you could simulate a TV interview or a radio interview) • You may wish to invite the customer relations officer from the supermarket to talk about popular foodstuffs • You may wish to invite a local baker to discuss bread/bread making • Food-tasting session
Lesson five/six: design	After collecting all the evidence required, ask the children to 'design' a sandwich. You may wish to do this as a recipe with a list of instructions
Lesson seven/eight: key skills	**Identification of key skills:** in this lesson children are given the opportunity to reflect, share and discuss their sandwich designs. The class will list the key skills they need to complete their project. Children should then be asked to assess their ability in each skill and then plans formulated to address these
Lesson eight/nine combined: make/ evaluation	**Health and safety:** food hygiene. **Make:** children to make the sandwich with their chosen filling and chosen bread (you may wish the children to make the bread). Invite the lighthouse keeper with his wife to taste and choose (can be more than one) a sandwich for his new lunches.

Things for you to consider in your evaluation of a lesson/unit of work:

- Was the context meaningful, exciting and engaging?
- Were the children able to select from a variety of materials?
- Did the children take risks?
- Did the children ask for reassurance?
- Did you allow enough time for each stage?
- What 'pitfalls' did the children encounter that could be addressed in the future?
- Were children able to self-assess and peer assess constructively? Did the children feel that their work was valued?

Things for children to reflect on at the end of a unit of work:

- Have I learned any new skills?
- Did I organise the given time well?
- Did I work in a safe way?
- Did I work well in a team?
- How did I respond when things did not go to plan?
- Did I ask questions when I did not understand?
- Did I use the right materials for my project?

Summary of key points

- Design & technology allows children to become part of the technological world.
- The engagement of children through a meaningful context within a safe environment is important to the success of a design & technology project.
- Children should be instilled with a curiosity as to how things work.
- Children should be given opportunities to research inventors and inventions, to develop a sense of the past, present and future.
- The five-stage process of a design & technology project is product analysis, design, key skills, make and evaluate.

References

Armitage, R. and Armitage, D. (1994) *The Lighthouse Keeper's Lunch.* London: Scholastic Hippo.

Bennett, T. (2014) I know therefore I can. *Times Educational Supplement*, 10 January, pp. 26–30.

Davies, L.T. (2004) *Meeting SEN in the Curriculum: Design & Technology.* London: David Fulton Publisher.

Department for Education (DfE) (2013) *The National Curriculum for England Framework Document.* London: DfE.

Ewens, T. (2014) *Reflective Primary Teaching.* Northwich: Critical Publishing.

Hay/McBer Group (2000) *Research into Teacher Effectiveness: A Model of Teacher Effectiveness.* DfEE Research Report 216. London: DfEE.

Miller, J. (2011) *What's Wrong with DT?* London: RSA.

Ofsted (2011) *Meeting Technical Challenges? Design and Technology 2007–10.* Manchester: Ofsted.

Ofsted (2012) *Ofsted's Subject Professional Development Materials: Design & Technology – A Training Resource for Teachers of Design & Technology in Primary Schools.* London: Ofsted.

Rose, J. (2009) *Independent Review of the Primary Curriculum: Final Report.* DCSF-00499–2009. London: DfES.

Wilson, A. (2011) *Creativity in Primary Education*, 2nd edn. Exeter: Learning Matters.

Online sources

Design & Technology Data (DATA) www.data.org (accessed August 2014)

Robinson, Sir Ken www.sirkenrobinson.com (accessed August 2014)

Wilton, G. (2014) Iterative design: the shape of the future of design technology, http://designfizzle.wordpress.com/2014/02/28/iterative-design-the-shape-of-the-future-of-design-technology/ (accessed August 2014)

5 Geography

Marion Hobbs

Geography is a compulsory subject in the National Curriculum, but that's not why we should teach it! Children are curious creatures and geography allows the inner explorer in each of us to emerge. Teaching geography should allow you and your class to embark on a shared journey of discovery about the world around you.

In the most recent geography subject reports, Ofsted identified that the quality of geography teaching is often judged to be inadequate but that slow progress is starting to be made (Ofsted 2004, 2011). The reasons for these findings are many and complex but a contributory factor is the lack of subject knowledge and understanding of pedagogy by teachers (Catling *et al.* 2007; Iwaskow 2013). Iwaskow (2013) found that, despite teachers having outstanding skills in the classroom, many were unable to plan and deliver outstanding geography lessons.

This chapter aims to use the three-lens model to address these issues. It will give an overview of subject knowledge, consider pedagogy and discuss the identity of geography. Finally, subject knowledge, identity and pedagogy will be combined in the geography teachers' toolkit, which will identify practical ideas to ensure that geography lessons become high-quality teaching and learning experiences both for children and their trainee teachers.

The identity of geography

Geography is a subject that can harness the curiosity of young children and help them to make sense of their surroundings. If you have ever spent an hour in the company of a preschool child you will know that one of the most frequent words you will hear is 'why'. Why is it raining when I want to play in the garden? Why do we have to go in the car to the shops? Why do I have to wear my hat and scarf today? Children are natural geographers, and geography teachers should harness this curiosity and build on it, to ensure that geography as a curriculum subject meets their needs. Geography is all about answering questions about the world around us, and explaining how and why environments – both natural and man-made – develop in a particular way.

Geography has two main strands: physical geography and human geography. Both human and physical geography share the common characteristics that distinguish geography as a subject. Studying places, examining spatial distributions, and communicating using maps and plans combine to give geography its unique identity (Scoffham 2010).

All geographical study should be rooted in place study. Teachers need an appreciation of children's place experiences to ensure planning and teaching are relevant and stimulating to children (Catling, 2003).

Similarly, geographers are concerned with distributions and would identify the distances between features identifying where they are in relation to one another.

Geographers have their own unique way to communicate, through the medium of maps. Maps identify both place and space information, and planned geographical work should always include using maps to determine location (place) and distribution (space).

The geography curriculum

The National Curriculum has one attainment target in both key stages; this states that pupils, by the end of each, should be able to know, understand and apply the matters, skills and processes in the relevant key stage (DfE 2013). There is no statutory guidance on how teachers determine if this has been achieved and thus the main form of assessment in geography will be formative. Schools will determine their own systems of assessment and will also make decisions on how progress in geography over a term or a year is summarised and reported to parents.

Aims of the geography National Curriculum

The National Curriculum identifies that the purpose of geography is to inspire and create a thirst for knowledge of places and the people who live in them. Teachers need to ensure that children are aware of both the natural and the physical world. In geography this is referred to as 'physical' and 'human' geography. Put simply, physical geography is concerned with the natural environment and human geography with man's interaction with his environment. It is important for children to know and understand this distinction. The National Curriculum aims to teach children how interactions occur between the physical and the human world, which change and develop over time or differ in different scales. Thus as children's knowledge increases so should their understanding of how the interactions of physical and human processes combine to form differing features and landscapes.

The National Curriculum Aims suggest that geographical study should be undertaken within a context. Children should explore the physical and human features of a location, and be able to name the features and processes that are combined in that context. For example, they should be able to describe how the physical processes, such as weathering and erosion, combine to form mountain features, and be able to locate and name these features using real examples. Thus learning is less abstract and based more on features that can be explored through fieldwork experiences, pictures, maps and the internet.

Children should be taught to collect, interpret and communicate geographical information in a number of ways. For geography this should include using and interpreting maps, diagrams, globes and geographical information systems (GIS).

Communicating geographical information is the final skill in the National Curriculum Aims. This can be done in a variety of ways but should include the use of maps and writing at length (DfE 2013). The National Curriculum Aims should underpin all planned work in geography.

Key Stage 1

At Key Stage 1, pupils should be introduced to specific geographical vocabulary for both human and physical geography topics. Using examples from their locality, the United Kingdom and the world, they should study physical and human geography, and should use a range of geographical skills including simple fieldwork. They should be able to use maps, atlases, globes, compass directions, aerial photographs, plans, basic map symbols and keys.

Specifically at Key Stage 1 they should be taught to name and locate the world's seven continents, five oceans, the four countries and capitals of the United Kingdom, and the names of the seas surrounding the United Kingdom.

Through the study of a small area of the United Kingdom and a small area of a contrasting non-European country, they should also be taught to recognise similarities and differences in both the physical and human geography of the two localities.

Geography teaching should also include a study of seasonal and daily weather within the United Kingdom and what the weather is like in the wider world, including being able to describe the weather at the Equator and the North and South Poles.

Key Stage 2

At Key Stage 2, the context for geographical study should be a region of the United Kingdom, a region in Europe, and a region in North or South America. Similarities and differences of the regions should be studied in both physical and human geographical topics.

Physical geography topics include climate zones, biomes and vegetation belts, rivers, mountains, volcanoes and earthquakes, and the water cycle.

Human geography topics include: types of settlement and land use, economic activity including trade links, and the distribution of natural resources including energy, food, minerals and water.

Specifically at Key Stage 2 children should be taught to name and locate counties and cities of the United Kingdom, geographical regions, and topographical features and land use patterns. They should know how these have changed over time. Focusing on Europe and North and South America, children should be able to identify countries, physical and human characteristics, and major cities. When studying these areas children need to understand the differences in time zones, and be able to recognise key lines of latitude and longitude including the Equator, Northern Hemisphere, Southern Hemisphere, Tropics of Cancer and Capricorn, Arctic and Antarctic Circle and the Prime Meridian.

Geographical skills and fieldwork should underpin work at Key Stage 2. All studies should include working with maps, atlases, globes and digital mapping. Ordnance Survey (OS) maps should be used, and four- and six-figure grid references should be taught. Children should be given opportunities to gather and use a range of data using fieldwork techniques.

It is important to go beyond the simple approach of rote learning of the physical and human geographical features identified in the National Curriculum, however tempting this may be when faced with a list of localities and features that should be taught. Skilful contextual planning that focuses on the aims of geography will ensure that children are taught in a meaningful way, and such planning needs to encapsulate the identity and pedagogy of geography.

Reflection points

- *What key places identified in the National Curriculum do I know least about?*
- *How can I start to develop my personal geographical knowledge of these places?*

The pedagogy of geography

Enquiry

Good geographical teaching is characterised by an enquiry-based approach that utilises high-quality resources to seek evidence to answer questions. Outstanding geographical lessons immerse the children in practical problem-solving activities that allow them to investigate problems and communicate answers in a variety of ways (Pickford, Garner and Jackson 2013). Where possible, fieldwork contributes to the enquiry, and real places provide context for young children to investigate and explore the world around them (Barlow 2013). In this section how geography should be taught is considered and the fundamental pedagogy of geography is explored.

Geographical enquiry harnesses the natural curiosity of children. Children have a real sense of awe and wonder about their surroundings, and geographical enquiry enables them to ask questions and seek answers to enable them to understand their environments (Barnes 2011).

Enquiry questions are the basic questions that children will research in a geography topic. Where is this place? What is it like? How did it become like this? We can use these questions as a basis for planning and to impose questions on the children, however it is far more effective if children can generate their own questions at the start of a topic. Once children take ownership of the questions they are far more curious to find the answers, and so put more effort into their geographical work (Scoffham 2013).

Encouraging children to be active in this way doesn't happen overnight and the enquiry approach needs to be embedded in the school geography policy (Wood 2013). The more children are exposed to this approach from an early age, the more they can develop skills of enquiry and an independent, problem-solving approach (Green *et al*. 2013).

Geographical skills

Outstanding geography lessons utilise geographical skills in a range of teaching strategies, and thus such lessons should feature mapping skills, interpretive skills and fieldwork.

Map work

Learning how to read a map is a lengthy process and something that needs to be planned by the whole school community. Children need to have access to maps at a very early age, and the conventions of map making and map reading need to be broken down and integrated throughout geographical teaching from nursery to Year 6. It is not the intention of this chapter to describe in detail how to teach mapping skills – these are covered in a number of detailed geographical publications (see, for example Bridge, cited in Schoffam 2010) – but to consider how such skills should be included in geography teaching and planning.

Maps are the unique way in which geographers communicate. Children do need to be taught how to read and use a map, but this shouldn't be done in isolation. Mapping skills should be integral to a geographical topic and children should be given opportunities to apply their mapping skills in real contexts. It is useful to compare learning to read a map with learning the skills in a competitive sport. The skill is introduced but opportunity is given to use the skill in a small group situation in the same lesson. Over a number of weeks the skill is developed until the full game can be played. When planning a geography topic, it is essential to consider what geographical skills can be introduced and applied in the first lesson and then built upon during subsequent lessons. At the end of the planned geography work the skill can be applied in other contexts.

Interpretation

Outstanding geography lessons are well resourced and provide children with a wide range of opportunities to use interpretive skills. Children need to be able to use evidence to solve problems, draw conclusions and summarise information. This evidence can come from a wide range of sources, including maps of all kinds, photographs, postcards, posters, information leaflets, information books, websites, television news clips, webcams, guest speakers, artefacts, guide books and holiday guides. This list is by no means exhaustive but gives an indication of some of the sources you can draw on when planning geography lessons. All lessons should allow children to interpret information and use resources as clues to answer enquiry questions. Not every child or group needs access to the same resources, and using differing resources for different groups and individuals can be a way to support differentiation. The important thing is that children are given an opportunity to study and reflect on the resources, and use them to support their problem-solving enquiries.

Fieldwork

There is no substitute for giving children real-world experiences and every opportunity to take children outside the confines of the classroom should be grasped. Introducing urban children to the delights of the natural world can be a real life-affirming experience. I will never forget the look of awe and wonder on the face of a streetwise Y6 who, seeing a waterfall for the very first time, described the plunge pool as being the top of a pint of beer. The quality of the work post-field trip was phenomenal and worth every minute of the lengthy time and preparation that fieldwork demands.

Fieldwork is an important component of geography and allows children to experience first hand the context of their studies (Holmes 2014). Fieldwork can support physical and human geography. It involves gathering data in a variety of ways to allow children to answer questions and make predictions about both human and natural environments (Richardson 2010). Good and regular fieldwork motivates pupils and enhances their learning (Ofsted 2011).

Fieldwork that supports knowledge about physical geography would involve children gathering data in the field (see Figure 5.1) to help them understand how the physical processes combine to form the features of the natural world. This could involve taking photographs, making sketches, measuring features and collecting data that can be used in the classroom to explore the physical features observed and explain how they have developed. Fieldwork that supports human geography should allow children to gain an understanding of how and why human features are located where they are and to understand the impact of these features on the environment and community in which they are located.

Outstanding geography planning combines an enquiry approach with a range of geographical skills in a real context; the next section of this chapter gives examples of this in the form of a geography teacher's toolkit.

Figure 5.1 Fieldwork at the coast

Reflection points

- *What geographical skills am I competent in?*
- *What geographical skills do I still need to learn?*
- *How can I develop my personal geographical skills so I am confident in using them in the classroom?*

The geography teacher's toolkit

This section aims to consider how a trainee teacher can combine subject knowledge and pedagogy to plan high-quality geography lessons. It will also share practical ideas for activities that would evidence the pedagogy of geography.

There is considerable flexibility within the National Curriculum to enable the selection of a range of places and themes to study. It makes sense when planning to consider how to combine elements of the curriculum together within a topic. This saves time and allows topics to be covered in context. As children are required to consider similarities and differences between places, a practical approach to enable this skill to develop is, with the youngest children, to start with topics focusing on the school and its locality. This allows children to construct meaning from a known environment and ensures that they have some reference points on which to make comparisons in later work. To ensure there is progression in the knowledge of the local area, it is useful to revisit the school locality with older children to enable deeper comparisons to be made between their own locality and other areas selected to study.

As a trainee teacher, your main focus will be on medium- and short-term planning but before developing plans to use during professional practice you should consult the school long-term outline plans, which will detail the themes, places and skills that are to be covered in each year group (Richardson 2010). It is important to consider the experiences and interests of the children and ensure work is planned that will build on previous work and knowledge that the children already have. Taking opportunities to talk to small groups of children from a range of abilities before planning work will be of great help to you in planning. Such discussions could be in the form of geographical games (Whyte 2013), which enable you to assess how the children use geographical skills, vocabulary and knowledge, and enable you to build on their existing levels of success.

Planning at Key Stage 1

When planning an enquiry for Key Stage 1, consideration of the following points will ensure that several elements of the National Curriculum are combined in the enquiry.

- What locality will I choose? Select from the local area, an area of the UK or a non-European locality.
- What fieldwork can be undertaken if the selected area is local or within the UK?
- What are the main physical and human features of this locality?

- How can I use maps, plans, globes and atlases to show the location of regions, cities, towns, oceans, seas, rivers, etc. that are significant to this locality?
- What is the weather like in this region? How can I use maps, plans, globes, and atlases to explore the weather patterns?
- What resources will I need to ensure children are able to pose and answer questions in an enquiry?
- What geographical vocabulary will I introduce?
- What are the differences between this locality and the local area? What are the similarities?

Planning at Key Stage 2

Similarly for Key Stage 2 the following will ensure that the National Curriculum is addressed in the enquiry.

- What region in the UK, Europe, North or South America will be the focus of the work?
- What fieldwork can I undertake to support the enquiry?
- Which of the following physical features could be included in the enquiry: climate zones and biomes; vegetation belts; rivers; mountains; volcanoes and earthquakes; the water cycle?
- Which of the following human features could be included in the enquiry: types of settlement; land use; economic activity; trade links; resource distribution?
- In a UK study, which counties, cities, topographic features and land use patterns can be included? Is it appropriate to include the location of the Prime Meridian?
- In a European or North/South American study, which major cities, time zones, lines of latitude and longitude (Equator, Tropics of Cancer and Capricorn, Arctic and Antarctic Circle, and Prime Meridian) can be included?
- What specific skills will I teach and use in the enquiry?
- What resources will be needed to ensure children are able to pose and answer questions in an enquiry?
- What new geographical vocabulary will be introduced and what can I build on from previous geography work?
- What are the differences between this locality and the local area? What are the similarities?

Answering the questions will give you a framework that will support the construction of medium- and short-term plans, and will also identify gaps in personal knowledge that need to be addressed before teaching the children. The Geographical Association (www.geography.org.uk) is an excellent starting point for information and online professional development. It produces a quarterly journal aimed at primary teachers that contains a wealth of ideas for lessons and many links to online resources. As a member you have access to back copies of the journal electronically and free access to all the resources.

Combining this researched information with an enquiry approach will ensure the development of high-quality medium- and short-term planning.

Generating questions in enquiry

Questions are fundamental to a geographical enquiry, and finding ways to ensure children themselves devise the enquiry questions is a key feature of outstanding geographical practice. Generating questions with the children can be done in a number of ways: hot seating, circle time, small-group discussions, role play, mind mapping, etc. The important point is that the children develop questions about what they want to know about a topic. A record should be made of the questions, which can be returned to at the end of the enquiry. Once questions have been generated, children should also be involved in considering how questions can be answered, and their suggestions noted. This may be through exploring websites, studying photographs, interviewing people, reading information books or leaflets, experimenting with practical equipment or undertaking fieldwork.

Once the questions and the methods for investigating have been agreed, children should be given time to investigate and find out the answers to their questions. This can be done individually, in pairs or in groups, depending on the group dynamics, previous experiences and existing knowledge of the children. When the children have found their answers, they need to communicate these to the rest of the group; again this can be done in a variety of ways, including posters, PowerPoints, poems, accounts, role play scenarios and demonstrations. The emphasis should be on the children sharing what they have found out with the rest of the class, including what they have concluded. This is an opportunity to revisit the original list of questions and determine if all the questions have been answered. It may be that more questions have been identified during the investigations and these can also be shared with the group.

Enquiry

Enquiries don't have to be large scale – they can be planned for one or two lessons or across a number of weeks. For example, a class may be asked about where to locate a new school bench. Enquiry questions can be generated by asking children what information they would need to know to ensure the bench is put in the best place. Likely questions could be: Should it be in the sun or shade? Who would like to use it? Should it be near where ball games are played? Does it need to be sheltered from wind or rain? Would it be useful for story time/outdoor lessons? Could it be useful for school team games? Children would need to gather evidence about different sites, and find out what other children and adults think, to answer these questions. Evidence could be generated by, for example, keeping weather records, making sketches, taking photographs, interviewing, and conducting surveys. The evidence would then need to be communicated to the rest of the class by presenting the information in a variety of ways, such as on posters, graphs, PowerPoints or written accounts. Finally a decision would be made based on all the evidence. During the investigation the children can use maps and plans; these can also be used in their presentations.

Geographical skills

All planned geographical work should identify appropriate skills that will be introduced and taught in the geographical topic. The specific skill will need to be introduced and taught but should be practised within the context of the topic.

The following example demonstrates how this approach could be used to support the skill of using grid references. Key Stage 1 children are required to study the physical and human geography of a small area of a non-European country. They are also required to use maps, plans, globes, basic map symbols and keys. This would be an opportunity to plan an enquiry into the named area and use a range of mapping skills to answer enquiry questions. To use the maps, plans and globes children need to be able to locate features. This is done by using grid coordinates.

When planning this topic it would be useful to identify the use of coordinates as a skill that will be introduced to the children and then built upon during the topic, culminating with the children using grid coordinates in their final session of the enquiry when they present their work to the class. The children should be taught how a grid system can be used to locate features. Grids can use alpha-numeric coordinates with letters on the vertical columns and numbers on the horizontal rows. Simple alpha-numeric combinations then identify the squares. Children can then locate the square and what feature is in it.

A useful way for children to experience using grids for location is to draw a large-scale grid on the playground and allow themselves to be labelled as numbers and letters. Games can then be played and children meet in the squares. A creative way to introduce a new area of study would be for the children to collect artefacts and pictures of the selected area during this playground grid game, which are then used throughout their enquiry as sources of evidence. Each source of evidence would give the children clues to use in their place study. These activities introduce and teach the skill of using grid squares for location, and they should be built upon during the place study enquiry. In subsequent lessons children should be given opportunities to use grids in simple atlases, and on appropriate globes and maps. When answering enquiry questions children should be set the success criteria of locating the features using grid references throughout the topic. For example, one group may be describing the natural features of the area and would identify using grid squares where these are in the region. At the end of the topic the children should be able to use their learned skill in subsequent topics and build on their skills by moving on to conventional four-figure grid references in later years.

Fieldwork

Fieldwork should be integral to planned geography as it allows children to gain first-hand experiences, and enables them to use and apply geographical skills. This can be in a range of contexts and scales. All fieldwork should be undertaken using appropriate risk assessments, and school and local authority guidance. You should refer to school policies and complete all the required paperwork before taking the children out of the classroom.

Rather than simply asking the children to observe and collect data, a more creative approach would be to set challenges for the children to work out. Divide the class into groups and provide each group with a statement about the local area. Statements could be:

- There are ten houses with a blue door in School Street
- There are five houses that have a Victorian date
- I would need to take a bus to buy the materials to paint my bathroom
- I can't buy the ingredients to make tomato soup from the local shops
- I would need to cross a busy road to buy the local paper
- If I walk for 15 minutes from the school I can take part in three different sports.

Provide maps and plans of the area and ask the children to plan how to prove if the statements are true. Fieldwork skills such as observation, note taking, sketching, tallying and interviewing would all be used within a problem-solving context, allowing children to apply their knowledge and skills in a purposeful way. Finally, children would use presentation and communication skills when sharing their conclusions with the class.

Combining enquiry, place study and skills

The following example suggests ideas for a study of Brazil in South America for Upper Key Stage 2 children. The ideas and activities can be adapted for other localities, features and ages.

Locality study: Brazil

A good way to introduce a locality study is to play a guessing game with the children. Arrive in the classroom with a suitcase or backpack filled with clues to the location. Split the class into teams and give each ten pieces of paper to write down their guesses. Take out each clue one by one and allow time for each group to ask a questions about it to which you can answer only yes or no. This encourages the children to construct deeper questions. After each round of questions allow each team to discuss where they think the location is and to write down their guess. Collect the guesses after each round. After the lesson you will have valuable formative assessment information as you will be able to see how quickly the children interpreted the information and what level they are working at in terms of geographical knowledge and vocabulary used in the questioning. Make the clues easier to interpret as the game continues.

This is an ideal opportunity to introduce geographical terms and features. For example, a clue could be an outline map of the world marked with the Tropics of Cancer and Capricorn and the information that the mystery country lies within these lines of latitude. Discussions and questions can then clarify what the lines are. Clues can include clothing, sun cream, airline tickets, holiday itineraries, pictures, key words in the country's language, maps and websites. This activity allows you to introduce the requirements of the National Curriculum in a fun way by including names of human and physical features, lines of latitude and longitude, and information about time zones, weather and biomes.

Once the name of the country has been established, challenge the children to write the longest address in the world. Allow access to atlases, globes and digital maps on iPad and computers. Ask the children to use the information to write the address of an imagined hotel. They should be challenged to not only name the street, area, city, region and country, but also to move on to a grander scale and include details such as the continent, hemisphere, next to which ocean, near to which other countries, and contained within which lines of latitude and longitude. Again this covers all the requirements of the National Curriculum but gives context and purpose.

The next stage of the topic should involve the children in determining their own enquiry questions. Hot seating is a good way to generate questions. Prime a 'volunteer' to role play being a primary-aged child in a school in Brazil. Ask this child to pretend to answer each question in broken English or by saying 'Eu nao entendo voce' ('I don't understand', in Portuguese). The aim is to establish that the children will need to research the questions. However, by asking a person rather than just being asked to volunteer questions, the children become much more inquisitive and creative.

All questions should be recorded and, after the session, grouped together to form a line of enquiry for a group or the class in later lessons. Typical questions could be: Who do you support in football/rugby? What's your favourite television programme? Have you got a … (substitute current favourite electronic games console)? What's your best subject at school? Where do you go shopping? Do you like … (substitute current favourite TV/music personality). Have you got a pet? What phone do you have? What car do you have? What's your house like? Where did you go on holiday? What's your favourite food? The list is endless and will always contain some surprises!

Once you have gathered the questions, you need to group them into areas for research. For example, questions about sports, television and films could be combined in the enquiry question, 'How do people in Rio de Janeiro/Brazil spend their leisure time?' 'Where do you go on holiday?' could be considered more broadly as an enquiry question about what you could do on holiday in Brazil. The result of the hot-seating activity therefore, would be to generate a range of geographical topics to research. Approaching the topic in this way fulfils the geographical aim of inspiring a thirst for knowledge about places and the people who live in them.

Once the research topics have been established, activities should be planned that combine geographical skills and knowledge, and allow children to seek answers to their enquiry questions. For example, using the sport questions, children could use maps, plans and digital mapping to locate on a map the football grounds used for the World Cup. Using OS maps, children could provide detailed information on the grid reference location of the city where each stadium is, and plan journeys to and from each one. Using the holiday research topic children would need to locate and describe the physical features of Brazil, the Amazon River, beaches, major cities and sites. In investigating the weather and leisure questions, children could plan itineraries and write guidance on what to wear, based on their findings about the weather in the country.

Other enquiries could focus on the features of rivers and identify these on the Amazon River, and biomes could be studied in the context of the Amazon forest.

Not all of these ideas need to be planned in one geographical topic – the specific selection of research themes would depend on the experiences and interests of the children and the long-term plans of the school.

Undertaking these activities would ensure that children are learning about climate and time zones, biomes and vegetation patterns, settlement patterns and distribution of

Figure 5.2 Exploring the features of rivers in the classroom

resources, and in doing so are using a wide range of geographical skills. Fieldwork could still be planned as there are several sites around the country – the Eden Project, for example – that offer experiences of rainforest, tropical and beach environments. Local rivers could be focused on and comparisons made with the River Amazon. Undertaking local fieldwork is another way of covering the requirement to consider similarities and differences between the selected study area and the local area.

Working in this way with young children is fun and exciting. It takes a lot of time and preparation but the effort is worth it, and the result is outstanding teaching and learning.

Reflection points

- *Select a village, town or country you are very familiar with and list the information you know about it.*
- *Using the planning guidance, plan a medium-term plan for KS1 or KS2.*
- *List the geographical skills you would need to be confident in.*
- *List the sources you could use to gather resources.*

Summary of key points

- Geography is a statuary subject in the National Curriculum.
- Geographers study both physical and human geography, and consider the interaction of the two in real-world contexts.
- Geographers are concerned with the study of places.
- Geographers use an enquiry approach to pose and answer questions.
- Geographers combine mapping skills, interpretation and fieldwork in problem-solving enquiries.
- Geography planning should combine skills, enquiry and place study.
- Whole-school geography should ensure good local knowledge is developed to allow children to identify similarity and difference.
- There are many approaches that can be taken in the teacher's toolkit, but providing practical, fun experiences will harness the natural curiosity children have in the wider world.

References

Barlow, A. (2013) Geography and history in the local area. In Scoffham, S. (ed.) *Teaching Geography Creatively*. Abingdon: Routledge, pp. 100–111.

Barnes, J. (2011) *Cross-Curricular Learning 3–14*, 2nd edn. London: Sage.

Catling, S. (2003) Curriculum contested: primary geography and social justice. *Geography*, 88, 3, pp. 164–210.

Catling, S., Bowles, R., Halocha, J., Martin, F. and Rawlinson, S. (2007) The state of geography in English primary schools. *Geography*, 92, 2, pp. 118–136.

Department for Education (DfE) (2013) *The National Curriculum for England Framework Document*. London: DfE.

Green, J., Shaw Hamilton, A., Walsh, M., O'Mahony, O. and Pike, S. (2013) On our own (with a bit of help). *Primary Geography*, Spring, pp. 28–29.

Holmes, S. (2014) Learning physical landscapes. *Primary Geography*, Spring, pp. 24–25.

Iwaskow, L. (2013) Inspiring curiosity and fascination. *Primary Geography*, Autumn, pp. 24–25.

Ofsted (2004) *Ofsted Subject Reports 2002/03: Geography in Primary Schools*. London: HMSO. Online at www.ofsted.gov.uk/resources/annual-report-200203-ofsted-subject-reports-primary (accessed August 2014).

Ofsted (2011) *Learning to Make a World of Difference: Subject Report Geography*. London: Ofsted.

Pickford, T., Garner, W. and Jackson, E. (2013) *Primary Humanities Learning through Enquiry*. London: Sage.

Richardson, P. (2010) Planning the curriculum. In Scoffham, S. (ed.) *Primary Geography Handbook*. Sheffield: Geographical Association, pp. 302–311.

Scoffham, S. (2010) Young geographers. In Scoffham, S. (ed.) *Primary Geography Handbook*. Sheffield: Geographical Association, pp. 15–23.

Scoffham, S. (2013) A question of research. *Primary Geography*, Spring, pp. 16–17.

Whyte, T. (2013) Fun and games in geography. In Scoffham, S. (ed.) *Teaching Geography Creatively*. Abingdon: Routledge, pp.14–30.

Wood, S. (2013) Progression in questioning skills. *Primary Geography*, Spring, pp. 22–23.

6 History

Chris Russell

History is an essential aspect of the primary curriculum. The story of the past defines us, our friends and families, and the places we live. History provides us with a sense of identity, pride and belonging. Our roots, both old and new, are founded on the footsteps of those that have gone before, their actions and their legacies. As such, history is the essence of one's being and therefore is an integral part of a balanced curriculum that is focused on producing well-informed children who are equipped for the world and the future ahead.

This chapter explores history and the three-lens model. History will be defined in terms of skills, concepts, and attitudes and values, as well as the theme of identity. Specific teaching approaches will be explored, such as enquiry and meaningful historic visits, as well as additional considerations such as interpretations of history and evidence.

The identity of history

The tag-line for the film *The History Boys* indicates that 'History is just one (bloody) thing after another', and while this could be argued as being the case, history is so much more than that. I often introduce the history sessions to the trainee teachers I work with by asking them 'What is history?' and then expanding upon this by asking 'What is primary history?' It doesn't take long for the trainees to identify words that define history as being 'the past', 'people', 'places' and 'events', and for that thought process to move on to include 'interpretations', 'bias', 'points of view', 'understanding', 'tolerance' and 'empathy'. The conversation then expands to looking at the curriculum document and picking out the historical skills, concepts, and attitudes and values that are associated with the subject of history.

Historical skills can be seen as including observation, sequencing, analysing, questioning, understanding, synthesising and communicating. Bloom's taxonomy (1956), or subsequent versions of it, can be used as a useful planning tool when devising and creating learning experiences, schemes of work and historical investigations.

Historical concepts include chronology, change, continuity, similarities and differences, evidence, cause and effect, and significance, while attitudes and values concern themselves with ideas of empathy, tolerance, understanding different points of view, and a sense of enthusiasm and curiosity.

Another aspect that defines history is that of identity. The sense of belonging that someone demonstrates for his or her hometown or adopted city can be a powerful driving force in their life. It is a notion that can define them as a person and their interests and outlook on life. The sense of pride is fascinating: some people will be proud of the strangest of things, simply because it is associated with their home and their roots. Identity can be explored in a variety of ways through the subject of history, helping children to explore who they are and where they fit in, in the world around them.

History, of course, can be many things, such as children's history, women's history, black history, post-war history, ancient history, family history and popular history. We can also investigate history in terms of a certain aspect or theme, such as the history of the Beatles or the history of association football.

History can be seen as not what happened but what someone in the past thought important enough to write down. The study of history is ever changing and is recognised as a subject in itself: historiography. However, as Black and MacRaild suggest, 'most people see history in terms of separate periods with each typified by a different way of life' (2007: 3). In more simple terms, history is the events of people in places in the past, and the study of history is a combination of these facts and the methods of how we know what happened in the past. It is a balance between content and enquiry.

Reflection points

- *What does history mean to you?*
- *How do you engage with the past?*
- *How does this impact upon your everyday life?*

The history curriculum

Debate surrounding the history curriculum somehow personifies our hopes and fears for the curriculum in general. Growing dissatisfaction with the Curriculum 2000 had led to much talk of 'areas of learning' being encouraged in schools, with some schools even being so bold as to rewrite plans and timetables to accommodate such changes. However, a change of government in 2010 and the *History for All* document in 2011 shifted the debate.

Ofsted's *History for All* report stated that children's understanding of chronology was 'no better than satisfactory', and asserted that teaching focused on knowledge and understanding rather than the concept of chronology. This was certainly the case. The same report stated that 'most pupils reached the end of Key Stage 2 with detailed knowledge derived from well-taught studies of individual topics'. While the teaching of history was 'good or better in most primary schools', this document can be seen as the starting point towards a shift in focus for the curriculum. The draft curriculum highlighted chronology as an important aspect and listed events that flowed from one to the next in telling the story of the past.

One criticism levelled at the draft curriculum for history was that it focused too heavily on British history, ignoring the rest of the world, such as Ancient Egypt. Others pointed towards the aspects of the curriculum that appeared to be removed from primary school history, such as the Victorians or learning about the Second World War at Key Stage 2. Others baulked at the number of events to be covered.

Such concerns were raised during the consultation period, and the curriculum that emerged in September 2013 for implementation the following year, while keeping some eyebrows firmly raised, did amend many of the follies of the original draft.

For example, Ancient Egypt was reinstated in the guise of a topic on 'the earliest civilizations', and accusations of being too British-centric were addressed with reference to 'the wider world' taking its place in the final wording. The chronological approach is clearly marked as ideal, but no longer compulsory, and while the primary curriculum at Key Stage 2 seemingly stops at 1066, there is scope to study a theme of history that goes beyond 1066 and could include such topics as the Victorians or the Second World War. A local study, equally, allows the potential for schools to explore events from the more recent past.

Topics such as the Tudors can be implemented in schools through studying 'the changing power of monarchs', as suggested in the 'non-statutory' guidance. The Victorians, and similarly the Second World War, might well be included in an individual school's curriculum through their local history study unit.

The wording of the final curriculum can be seen as being an encouragement for teachers to create learning experiences that 'inspire pupils' and encourage 'perceptive questions', and for the children to have the opportunity to 'think critically, weigh evidence and sift arguments'. This is a far cry from the feared fact list that many imagined.

With an emphasis on chronology and historical perspective, the curriculum at Key Stage 2 can also be seen as promoting the stories of the eras that are being studied. This helps develop understanding of one era blending into the next. This is perhaps best demonstrated when looking at the Viking and Anglo-Saxon struggle for the kingdom of England, where stories of intrigue, battles and political manoeuvring will capture the imagination of the children.

The curriculum underpins the importance of historical skills by stating that all pupils should 'understand the methods of historical enquiry'; this is to include understanding how 'interpretations of the past have been constructed'. While this may be a little ungracious towards practitioners who have for years shunned jaded textbooks in favour of an approach that looked to provide investigations and the use of evidence in their lessons, it is good to see this good practice embedded in the curriculum.

At Key Stage 1, it can be argued that there is little change at all between National Curriculum 2000 and the 2014 Curriculum. When looking at significant people, the curriculum suggests pairings such as Christopher Columbus and Neil Armstrong in comparing aspects of life in different periods and the impact these people had on the world around them. This is a potentially exciting area of study as is the proposed pairing of William Caxton and Tim Berners-Lee. While this might provide a more focused approach for some schools, it should be noted that the suggested figures for study are non-statutory and that not all units looking at significant lives need to be a comparison – the document mentions 'some'. The final choice is down to the school. Similarly, the choice of event that goes beyond living memory is at the discretion of the school. The curriculum itself suggests the Great Fire of London or the first aeroplane flight, or events that are commemorated through festivals or anniversaries. Several topics suitable for study present themselves at this point. It is imaginable that most schools will continue to examine Remembrance Day.

Of course, this has implications for the plotting and planning of the curriculum map for history. It is not extraordinary to imagine that schools would want to focus on Remembrance Day during the autumn term, when a local and national focus on remembrance commemorations is in evidence. The question, then, is where do all the other topics go and how does a school ensure coverage of all the topics? A simple search online will provide several examples of how some schools have set about this task.

One suggested curriculum map could look like Table 6.1 and is described below.

Key Stage 1 curriculum map

Key Stage 1 rationale: the gaps in the spring term for both Year 1 and Year 2 provide some flexibility. Teachers can use that time to develop schemes of work or, as is the case with the lives of significant individuals, this might provide the opportunity to study other people. Events beyond living memory are included in the autumn term, but here again the opportunity to study more than one event could be accommodated within the blank spaces.

Key Stage 2 curriculum map

Key Stage 2 rationale: as with Key Stage 1, the gaps in the example shown here as Table 6.2 provide opportunities for topics to be expanded upon. For instance, in Year 4, schools may like to develop the topic on the Romans to look at Roman society and culture in a way that goes beyond looking at the impact of the Romans upon Britain. The units that specifically address British history have been placed in chronological order, which should help develop the chronological understanding highlighted earlier in this chapter. In addition, Year 6 have the option to develop additional topics and units of study, particularly after the SATs tests in May. This could be a return to the local history unit or even an

Table 6.1 Key Stage 1 history curriculum map

	Autumn	Spring	Summer
Year 1	Changes within living memory		Significant historical events, people and places in their own locality
Year 2	Events beyond living memory		Lives of significant individuals

Table 6.2 Key Stage 2 history curriculum map

	Autumn	Spring	Summer
Year 3	Achievements of earliest civilisations	Ancient Greece	Changes in Britain from the Stone Age to Iron Age
Year 4	Roman Empire and its impact on Britain		Britain's settlement by Anglo-Saxons and Scots
Year 5	Viking and Anglo-Saxon struggle for the kingdom of England	Local history study	Study of an aspect or theme
Year 6	A non-European society		

in-depth study of a significant person. It should be remembered that the National Curriculum is a minimum requirement and that schools can add to the units as they see fit.

In fact the nine units identified at Key Stage 2 for study almost invite schools to provide an additional three units in order to have one unit for each term. Schools with split classes will of course be adept at creating a two-year rotation in order to provide full coverage for their learners.

Reflection points

- *How you match units of work to the year groups can vary widely from school to school.*
- *What influences do you think there are that impact upon such decisions?*

The pedagogy of history

The pedagogy, or the principles of teaching history, can make or break your lessons and schemes of work. History as a subject is often associated with the dull and dry cartoon image of a boring lesson, where children are required to learn lists of names and dates with no hint of reason or purpose. Your experiences of history lessons might not quite fit this image. Maybe your experiences of sitting in a classroom centred around writing, using the history topic as a starting point for a piece of writing. Maybe you wrote about being a Victorian or what life was like at the court of Henry VIII. You may well have encountered comprehension tasks and cloze procedure exercises. It is easy to see that this is not the ideal inspirational approach to teaching history that we desire.

Of course, outstanding teachers have always strived to provide interesting, exciting and memorable lessons for the children in their classes. A purposeful lesson is the main aim, and this is arguably best achieved with lessons that are structured, considered and pitched correctly in order to challenge and inspire the children.

The curriculum document itself provides us with clues as to how best to teach history – although not compulsory, the document talks about pupils gaining a chronological narrative, chronology being a significant shift in the focus of the history curriculum, as we saw earlier. Hodkinson (2004) confirms that children retain more information if they have developed an understanding of chronology.

The aim of the curriculum document infers that children should 'gain and deploy' an understanding of abstract terms such as 'empire', 'civilization', 'parliament' and 'peasantry'. These are suggested terms, and so teachers are at liberty to develop these terms to suit the units they create, shape and deliver in their schools. The aims of the curriculum also highlight historical concepts, citing 'continuity and change, cause and consequence, similarity and difference and significance' as suggested areas to focus on, with the welcome outcome of the children's ability to 'make connections, draw contrasts, analyse trends and frame historically valid questions'. The children are also expected to 'create their own structured accounts', which includes written narratives. This provides the focus for teachers to include links to their English writing.

Enquiry is a cornerstone of good history investigations. It is explicitly referred to in the curriculum document. The aims of the curriculum require the pupils to 'understand the methods of historical enquiry'. Children are encouraged to use evidence rigorously in order to make historical claims and understand how some 'contrasting arguments' and 'interpretations of the past' have been constructed. This involves the consistent use of artefacts, documentary evidence, oral accounts and other kinds of evidence that are available, and then taking this further and challenging the children to make deductions and inferences, and rigorously explore the evidence set before them. In so doing, the children will address aspects of the curriculum such as sifting arguments and weighing evidence, as well as developing perspective and judgement.

The use of enquiry is advocated by Hilary Cooper (2013) and supported by organisations such as the Schools History Project (SHP). Interpretation of the curriculum document, as we have seen, allows for teachers to design investigations using a number of sources. By sources, we mean primary sources – artefacts of the time. Secondary sources, of course, have their uses and can provide interesting insights into the lives of people of the past, however the experience of using real artefacts, exploring their stories, making deductions and putting together the clues from the past helps make historical investigations come alive.

In order for a trainee teacher, or indeed teacher, to manage the requirements of the curriculum, it is necessary to sort, organise and define the skills and levels of understanding of the children in their school.

The curriculum has abandoned attainment targets as such. Instead the levels that schools have previously been working with have been replaced by a single statement, which indicates that 'by the end of each key stage, pupils are expected to know, apply and understand the matters, skills and processes specified in the relevant programme of study'. This has left many wondering just how they are expected to manage the curriculum with such an open-ended statement – and indeed a statement that refers to other curriculum areas.

Some schools may well maintain a system similar to that they have worked with in the past. However, other schools and their history coordinators will no doubt look to improve their existing practices and grasp the chance to investigate the opportunities presented by a change in the curriculum. The starting point for such an exercise would be the aims of the National Curriculum for history and the key skills that schools wish their children to develop over the course of their studies. We also need to consider the areas of history that we want the children to engage with, these primarily being knowledge and understanding, chronological understanding, enquiry, interpretation and communication.

In Table 6.3 I have created a grid that matches the aims of the National Curriculum for history to the specific aspects of history to be covered. I have identified skills or attributes for each area.

Table 6.3   Aims of the curriculum

Aims of the curriculum	Aspect of history	Skills and attributes
Pupils know and understand the history (of) how people's lives have shaped this nation and how Britain has influenced and been influenced by the wider world Know and understand the significant aspects of the history of the wider world, the nature of ancient civilisations, the expansion and dissolution of empires, characteristic features of past non-European societies, achievements and follies of mankind Understand historical concepts such as continuity and change, cause and consequence, similarity, difference and significance	Knowledge and understanding	Describe Explain Make links Compare
Pupils have a coherent, chronological narrative, from the earliest times to the present day Gain a historical perspective between short- and long-term time scales	Chronological understanding	Use of vocabulary relating to time Order Sequence Reason
Pupils understand the methods of historical enquiry, including how evidence is used rigorously to make historical claims Make connections, draw contrasts, analyse trends, frame historically valid questions	Enquiry	Use of primary sources Enquiry Questioning Reasoning
Pupils understand how evidence is used to make historical claims, and discern how and why contrasting arguments and interpretations of the past have been constructed	Historical interpretation	Interpretation Explaining Reasoning
Pupils place their growing knowledge into different contexts: understanding the connections between local, regional, national and international history; between cultural, economic, military, political, religious and social history Pupils gain and deploy a historically grounded understanding of abstract terms such as 'empire', 'civilisation', 'parliament' and 'peasantry'	Communication and organisation	Select Organise Communicate Present

The next step is to create a 'progression of skills table'. This could be used for planning as well as assessing children's achievements. It also gives the teacher the opportunity to ensure that the children have opportunities to 'ask perceptive questions, think critically, weigh evidence, sift arguments and develop perspective and judgement'.

Reflection point

- *When designing your lessons, how can you ensure that the skills address progression?*

The history teacher's toolkit

The history teacher's toolkit is a set of ideas and techniques that can be used in the classroom as part of your lessons. The important thing to remember is that each activity needs to centre upon a particular focus, skill, concept, or attitude or value of history.

This section provides you with a number of ideas that you could use in the classroom. Each can be tweaked to suit the needs, abilities and age range of the children in your class, making each activity a bespoke learning experience for them.

Historical trips

Some subjects are forever associated in your mind with a specific type of memory. History, in a lot of people's minds, is always associated with the school trip. Of course, this isn't always the case, but more often than not the reason for a school trip in the primary school is the history topic that is being studied at the time.

The important things to consider, when planning a historical trip, are many and varied. First, you need to identify the place you want to visit; this should be determined through a series of factors to do with your learning objectives and the opportunities available at the site. Ideally, the intended museum, gallery, stately home or historical site can offer something that you couldn't otherwise accomplish back in the classroom. This might be a specific objective, or the opportunity to see and maybe handle real artefacts, or talk to experts or eyewitnesses. Second, you need not only to consider the educational purpose of the trip, but also who will lead the activities and learning during the day. In lots of cases, that will be the teacher, however many sites and attractions cater for school trips and will have education officers who will lead sessions and take activities. Of course, provision changes from site to site, and you will have explored these opportunities when talking to the education officer and planning your visit.

It is important that the children know that the trip is part of their learning and, while it will be exciting and out of the ordinary, it should not be viewed as a day out or a treat. For that reason, the scheduling of the visit in your scheme of work is an important consideration. If the trip occurs early in the scheme of work, you need to consider how you will ensure that the children have enough knowledge to engage with the materials and benefit from the experts at the site. Similarly, a visit that is scheduled in the last week of a scheme of work sends out signals that this isn't an important part of the learning and that the unit is effectively over. There are pros and cons for scheduling the visit at any point in your scheme of work, however one thing you as the teacher must ensure is that you have communicated with the staff at the site and that they know where your children are at, in terms of their prior learning. This will help staff pitch their questions effectively and provide activities that, while challenging for the children, are accessible for them too. This adds to the overall beneficial qualities of the day.

Children like to know what is expected of them in any learning situation. This is most commonly seen in the classroom when the teacher is asked 'Am I doing it right?' or indeed 'What do I do?' Therefore, it is important that the children understand why they are going on a trip and what they will be doing when they get there. At this stage, the children may be introduced to the project or work that they will complete when they get back to class after the trip. This will also emphasise the focus for the visit. Preparation for the trip begins back at school, and may include historical information and background knowledge of the topic and the site to be visited. This will help the children make sense of the day and the trip a success. However, sometimes the prior knowledge that the children need may be more practical. For instance, imagine the aim of the trip is for the children to produce a documentary-style television programme or a podcast – the children will need to know how to use the recording equipment, the digital cameras and the video cameras. You certainly do not want to waste valuable time at the site demonstrating how to use a voice recorder, which could easily have been addressed back at school.

The children can use historical visits as the focus for their writing, or, as we have seen, a project that incorporates other areas of the curriculum, such as computing. One activity that requires the children to focus on gaining specific information on the day is to take along a teddy bear or a Lego man, or some other such suitable character. The children are challenged to take photographs of the character in different places around the site during the day. For instance, in a National Trust property, this could include the great hall, the drawing room, the parlour, the study, the gun room, the dining room, the bedroom and the kitchen. For each area, the children need to collect the relevant information in terms of 'What would have happened in this room?', 'What is kept in this room?' and 'How is cooking different here than in your house?' There are plenty of ways in which the children could find out that information, such as the guidebook for the property, or from a room steward or education officer. The children, back in school, compile a guidebook for the property as told by the teddy bear or Lego man. This provides a nice purpose for the day, and encourages the children to engage with the site in a creative and interesting way. The end product reveals the children's success and can be shared with the rest of the class, other classes in school and even parents on parents' evening.

Chronology

Chronology is a difficult concept for children to understand. They will often have a sense of time but not necessarily a sense of the depth of time. When I volunteered at Speke Hall, a National Trust property in Liverpool, it was my job to lead school trips around the property. However, first we needed to go back in time. In order to do this, I encouraged the class – and the teachers, too – to take a giant step. I usually did this in the gardens before entering the house. Each step took the class back 100 years. With each step I would ask questions such as, 'What year is it now?', 'Have you been born yet?', 'Has your school been built yet?', 'What do clothes look like?' and 'Are cars invented yet?' Within four steps we were back to Tudor times. This was to help the children recognise that the focus for the day was hundreds of years in the past, that life was clearly different for the people of that time, and that things we take for granted are not the same. It is worth noting that this activity works just as well at school as in the grounds of a stately home.

Timelines

Timelines are another classroom favourite for investigating chronology and a sense of time. Detractors will highlight the potential shortcomings of course, and using timelines, they will argue, may never truly help convey a sense of depth of time over thousands of years. However, they work nicely in investigating the recent past or a set number of years within a given period and in at least providing a starting point for developing a deep understanding of chronology.

In using timelines, children can order objects and sequence events, and they can create their own timelines using artefacts, objects and pieces of evidence. They can investigate given timelines, make deductions and answer questions. They can make statements about the past and begin to argue and reason as to why they have placed objects or events in a particular sequence. One activity could see the children given flash cards with details about a particular period or subject. The children then need to create a human timeline by asking questions and deducing information in order to place themselves in the correct order. In taking part in a timeline activity, the children are developing their chronological understanding, their reasoning ability and the skill of asking historical questions.

Primary resources

A Greek pot (or a replica, if a real one isn't to hand) can provide a gateway into the time of the Ancient Greeks. Simple questioning of the children, as they look at the pot, will lead to a great deal of information. This could not only include information about the pot itself and what it was originally made for, but also gathered from the images around the side of the pot. This could include assertions about the clothes the Greeks wore, their habits, lifestyle, hairstyle, food, living arrangements and religion. The children then put together their new understanding of life in Ancient Greece. From here, the children can test their ideas by looking at other pots, or could investigate aspects of history such as change and continuity and similarity and difference. This has all stemmed from asking simple questions. For example, the teacher can guide the investigation and the thoughts of the class by asking 'Who are these people?' This may lead to ideas about family life, which would then lead to asking 'What are they doing?' They might be celebrating, or bidding farewell in which case the investigation can explore ideas of empathy by asking 'How they are feeling?' The options are endless.

A nice twist to this activity is to challenge the children to think about what the people on the pot would otherwise be doing. Were they buying food for the party, or feeling sad about the farewell? Were they exercising, cleaning or hunting? The responses are endless and, again, can be used to explore comparisons of then and now.

This activity works just as well with a photograph of a resource.

Then and now

Looking at the concept of change and continuity is a good starting point for any historical investigation. Even the most alien of subject matters, such as Skara Brae, provides us with a peg for hanging our history investigations on. Photographs of Skara Brae reveal that people slept in what looks like a bedstead – a squared-off frame that could be stacked with animal skins to form a comfortable sleeping quarter. There is a clear fireplace, a contained fire for the people to sit around, cook and stay warm. Perhaps most curiously, the people seemed to have shelves and areas for keeping prized possessions and valuable items. The opportunities for investigating questions about then and now suddenly reveal themselves.

Investigations into the past often start with a comparison and simple observations. In this case, the children can consider their prized possessions and think about where they keep them. Children are encouraged to think about how they look after their belongings and how their prized possessions are treated differently to the other things that they own. Discussion here could easily lead to investigations about identity and belonging. Challenging the children to consider what is important to them and why the things they chose are more important than others, and then considering and comparing the types of things people at Skara Brae might keep on their shelves and why those things were important to them. As we have seen, exploring identity and belonging is an important aspect of history and begins to explain why history is an important subject for children to study.

Historical imagination/empathy

The word empathy does not appear in the curriculum document and yet it is a worthy aspect of history to study. The use of historical imagination enables the children to develop a sense of empathy and deepen their sense of understanding about the people of the past. A connection between the learner and the subject is vital. Understanding why someone did something or said something is different to knowing that it happened. There are a number of ways in which empathy could be addressed in the classroom. Using portraits or photographs and a series of questions is a tried-and-tested method of developing a sense of empathy. A portrait of a historical figure or a local citizen can be shown to the class, and the children challenged to consider what this person was thinking or feeling at a certain point. The use of an interactive whiteboard allows the children to share their thoughts quickly and easily with the rest of the class and makes an excellent starting point for work on this aspect of history.

An alternative approach to teaching this historical aspect is to share a picture of the historical figure and allude to a time in that person's life. For example, Winston Churchill on the eve of D-Day, or Henry VIII at the moment Anne Boleyn is executed. Instead of asking the straightforward 'How are they feeling?' question, challenge the children to think of a time when they have felt some of the feelings that the person being studied may be feeling at that point. It is unlikely that any of the children in your class will have ordered the execution of their wife, but they may have had feelings of remorse, stubbornness, grief and frustration that might be attributed to Henry VIII at that point in time. This can then be added to when it is revealed that Henry was hunting at the very moment Anne was executed and that, within a couple of days, he was engaged to Jane Seymour. This might influence the children's perceptions as to how he was feeling and how he felt towards the events and the people concerned.

The suitcase activity

The suitcase activity is based on the idea of the children using evidence to piece together an overall picture of a person, based upon the clues that are to be found contained within their suitcase. This is an activity that encourages the children to ask questions and to question presumptions. For instance, the suitcase I use for this activity contains a number of clues that point towards a Second World War pilot. There are a number of aviation clues, such as collectable cigarette cards of types of planes, a bomber jacket and evidence of journeys to far-flung places. However, nothing actually proves that the owner was a pilot. There are other clues as to gender, age and place of birth but, in all cases, there is no conclusive proof. The children are encouraged to think about the evidence in terms of three categories: things they know for sure, things they think they know and finally a question they would ask should the owner walk into the classroom. This process, and the discussion afterwards, reveals the need for caution when looking at evidence, and that interpretation and inference can play a large part in our perceptions of the world around us.

The problem

A useful approach when designing interesting learning experiences for the children is to pose a problem or set a challenge for them to solve. A successful activity here centres around a Greek pot. The children need to correctly identify the images on the pot using clues and evidence. At this stage I usually have a Greek pot covered in a cloth in the room. The children are informed that the pot is decorated with a picture of a Greek god or goddess. Their job is to find out which god or goddess is on the pot. To do this, each child is given a pack of information about a different god or goddess. Their job is to share the information with the other children on their table. As each child has information on a different god or goddess, this process is often best done by creating a poster containing all the information from all the children on the table. Each table in the room completes this task. The next step is for each child from each table to find out about the other Greek gods and goddesses on all the other tables in the room. This involves the children going to different tables and collecting the information from all the other posters that have been created. This having been completed, the children can return to their table and then be shown the pot. Having found out all the information in the room, the children can correctly identify the character depicted on the pot.

This section has looked at a number of strategies and approaches that can be used in the classroom or while on a historical visit. Each activity can be adapted to suit the age, abilities and bespoke needs of the children in your class. I very much hope that you will try these activities and make them your own, adding your own ideas and creating valuable learning experiences for the children in your class.

Summary of key points

Within this chapter we have:

- recognised the current place of history in the curriculum
- explored a rationale for the curriculum through exploration of themes, aspects and the unique characteristics of history
- begun to see how history is a vital and influential subject in the primary school
- explored concepts, such as chronology, change, continuity, evidence and significance
- explored values, such as tolerance and empathy, and underpinned these through approaches to teaching, such as enquiry
- recognised the importance of the progression of historical skills and attributes
- explored how history can enable and equip children to understand and live in the world around them
- emphasised how history is one of the most vibrant and engaging subjects in the primary curriculum.

References

Black, J. and MacRaild, D. (2007) *Studying History*. Basingstoke: Palgrave.

Bloom, B. (1956) *Taxonomy of Educational Objectives. The Classification of Educational Goals*. London: Longman.

Cooper, H. (2013) *History 5–11. A Guide for Teachers*, 2nd edn. Abingdon: Routledge.

Hodkinson, A. (2004) The social context and the assimilation of historical concepts: an indicator of academic performance or unreliable metric? *Research in Education*, 71, pp. 50–66.

7 Languages

David Barker

Foreign languages are a relatively new addition to the curriculum timetable in the primary school. Their introduction as a subject into Key Stage 2 is clearly not without challenge; training staff to deliver confidently the content of the programme of study is one of the key issues that schools face. However, the benefits of language learning are clear in a world where people can move more freely than ever between countries. The ability to understand other cultures and their practices is greatly assisted if individuals have a command of the language spoken by the citizens of those countries.

This chapter explores languages in the primary National Curriculum using the three-lens approach. It offers practical ideas that can be employed in the classroom to help children become confident language learners.

The identity of languages

Foreign languages in the primary school can open children's eyes to the world of speakers of other languages. At every step of learning a foreign language children should make comparisons with their mother tongue. Language teaching should draw on the best that primary teaching offers: a child-centred, multi-sensory approach to learning that guarantees progression and continuity, and secures learning outcomes because the children find language learning fun and interesting. Being able to communicate through the four skills of speaking, listening, reading and writing is fundamental to human experience; this experience is enhanced by the ability to be able to communicate in another language. The National Curriculum identifies one purpose of language learning to be able to read great literature in the language; a laudable aim indeed. However, being able to converse with foreign language speakers is an achievement that is highly motivating to young learners in these days of modern communication technologies.

Primary foreign languages is a subject that is very interactive and involves the use of lots of props, singing, simple texts, acting and role play, video and the internet. The children also learn grammar in fun and exciting ways, which reinforces their learning in English lessons. For grammar to be taught most effectively there needs to be an alignment of the English curriculum for grammar with the foreign language curriculum for grammar so that the pupils can be helped to make sense of how language works in both first and second languages. The Key Stage 2 Framework for Languages also promotes language learning strategies as a key ingredient in supporting effective language learning; the strategies are also applicable to other subjects in the curriculum. Strategies to help learning include the use of actions, rhyme, repetition, memory work, phonic understanding, dictionaries, contextual clues, discussion of language learning and language practice.

Primary school teachers are well placed to use their skills in delivering other curriculum subjects to help them to teach foreign languages. An awareness of the teaching of phonics in English; of spelling strategies such as 'look, say, cover, write, check'; of word, sentence and text-level work borrowed from the National Literacy Strategy – all of these can be used to help teach foreign languages. If parent helpers are native speakers of the foreign language, they can be a very useful support for checking resources that teachers prepare, as well as supporting the delivery of the lesson.

One interesting feature of teaching foreign languages in the primary school is the possibility of incorporating language teaching into other curriculum subjects. Foreign languages is the subject par excellence for creating cross-curricular links. Teachers can, if they are confident and competent enough in their language skills, deliver teaching of part of a curriculum subject in the target language. A useful way of practising numbers in the foreign language is through a 'mental/oral starter', which also develops at the same time as the children's understanding of the mathematical operation being practised. Rather than 'seven times four', use 'sept fois quatre'. The children can use individual whiteboards to show the answer, demonstrating their understanding of both the language and the mathematical operation. This way of working is related to CLIL (Content and Language Integrated Learning) an approach to language learning that is applied to real-life teaching and learning situations (Coyle, Hood and Marsh 2010). The Association for Language Learning promotes this approach as FLAME (Future for Languages as a Medium of Education).

Identity is an intrinsic part of language learning. Through learning another language, learners may also find out about the cultural practices of native speakers. The Languages document speaks of language education being 'a liberation from insularity'; it 'should foster pupils' curiosity and deepen their understanding of the world' (DfE 2013: 193). Byram and Doyé (1999) identify two contexts that influence the content of a curriculum, at micro and macro level. The curriculum is a reflection of the social, economic and political context within which the education system operates and Languages at Key Stage 2 mirrors this macro-context. There is also a micro-context that is of particular importance within each school: the choice of foreign language(s), how languages are taught, the timetabling of language teaching and the specific content chosen for the pupils in each year group will all help to create an individual identity for languages in each school.

To fully understand the cultural aspect of language learning, children need to be exposed to the cultural artefacts, customs, symbols and way of life of the native speakers of the language studied. The use of new technologies that can bring children in contact in real time with partner schools abroad helps to make language learning more purposeful and can give an insight into the daily lives of the native speakers of the target language who might live hundreds, if not thousands, of miles away. It is through an understanding of the notion of 'otherness' that children become more aware of their own cultural identities.

An understanding of identity in language learning is often referred to as Intercultural Understanding (in the Key Stage 2 Framework for Languages, 2007) or intercultural competence (Byram and Doyé, in Driscoll and Frost 1999; Jones and Coffey 2006). If the reasons for studying a language in the curriculum are purely utilitarian, native speakers of English might not be motivated to learn other languages because of the dominance of English worldwide as *lingua franca*. But language is also an expression of cultural identity. Jones and Coffey (2006: 140) differentiate between Culture and culture in a language learning context. Culture (capital 'C') refers to those characters and events from history remembered by the speakers of a language community – characters as diverse as writers, scientists, artists, kings and queens, politicians, etc., and events often of national significance marked by celebrations in the calendar. Culture with a capital 'C' can provide interesting lessons that help children to appreciate difference between language communities. Culture with a small 'c' refers to the daily customs of the speakers of the target language. This would include eating habits, school life and family life. If the children compare and contrast daily habits of target language speakers with their own daily practices, teachers can help children to develop an open mind towards the notion of 'otherness' as well as being made aware of 'sameness'.

It is clear that, to have an understanding of cultural identity of one's own and of the speakers of the target language requires a pedagogy that encourages questioning and critical analysis, and requires careful planning of cultural input. It is most likely that young children in the primary school are still developing in their own understanding of their cultural identity, which is dependent upon maturity and life experiences. In the 'Purpose of study' section in the National Curriculum there is reference to cultural awareness, but the ' Aims' and 'Subject content' sections are devoid of any reference to culture. This is regrettable since intercultural understanding is a very useful vehicle for assisting language learning; this is one aspect of the identity of languages that is threatened by the 2014 National Curriculum, ironically so now that languages are finally compulsory.

Reflection point

- *Think about your own experiences of learning a second language at school. What helped you to learn? What did you like/not like in your learning experiences? How will your experiences inform your practice?*

The languages curriculum

The inclusion of languages in the primary National Curriculum at Key Stage 2 from September 2014 elevates the status of the subject in the junior school phase (for the first time since the inception of the National Curriculum in 1988) to that of foundation subject, alongside art, D&T, geography, history, etc. The significance of this change of status cannot be underestimated; it represents a major shift in educational policy that gained impetus in the first decade of the twenty-first century. The comprehensive report by the Nuffield Foundation, *Languages: The Next Generation* (Nuffield Foundation 2000), highlighted the issues in language learning at all stages of schooling, and brought attention to the provision of language teaching in the primary phase. This was followed by the government's action plan for languages, Languages for All, Languages for Life (2002), which had entitlement to learning a foreign language in Key Stage 2 as a centrepiece of its strategy. In 2003 the Pathfinder Projects began; 19 local authorities were funded by the government to promote language learning in Key Stage 2. Of particular importance in supporting the introduction of foreign languages into primary schools was the publication of the content free Key Stage 2 Framework for Languages (DfES 2005). This planning framework organised learning across each of the year groups from Year 3 to Year 6. Teachers could use the topic-driven QCA schemes for French, German and Spanish (Qualifications and Curriculum Authority 2007) for support with language content and ideas for teaching.

The Dearing Review (Dearing and King 2007) called for foreign language learning to have compulsory status in the primary phase; this was accepted by a government White Paper, which fixed 2011 for this to become law. However the Coalition government brought about its own review of the National Curriculum in 2010. The proposals brought about by the previous Labour administration were abandoned as was the statutory status for languages in the primary curriculum. However, the Expert Panel set up in 2011 proposed that languages should be included in the primary curriculum. The final version of the languages curriculum 2013 established foreign languages as a foundation subject, and gave the profession control over choice of language and methodology.

There is lack of clarity, however, in the wording of the document. It is unclear whether community languages are to be included under the rubric of 'languages'. Substantial progress in one language is highlighted in the subject content part of the National Curriculum document, which implies that learning different languages is not an expectation at Key Stage 2, even though such an approach can be a rewarding experience for the children. There is no definition of 'substantial progress'.

According to the Languages Trends Survey 2013/14 conducted by the CfBT Education Trust with the British Council (CfBT Education Trust 2014), 95 per cent of 3,000 state primary schools taught a foreign language as part of the timetable in Key Stage 2, but the report raised doubts about the ability of the primary sector workforce to teach the requirements of the programmes of study (especially in Years 5 and 6), with 24 per cent of respondents having a language qualification at nothing more than GCSE level. However, the research also highlights a low level of engagement with CPD for foreign languages. The quantity of provision reported also raises doubts over schools' ability to fully deliver the requirements of the new languages curriculum.

The challenges facing primary school teachers cannot be underestimated. At Key Stage 2 the subject is titled 'foreign language' compared with 'modern foreign language' at Key Stage 3 (DfE 2013: 7). Primary school pupils will have the opportunity to study an ancient language that does not figure as part of the Key Stage 3 curriculum; this raises real questions about the value of teaching languages that the pupils will not be able to continue to learn in high school. Although primary practitioners may not have to face issues in pronunciation that they may face with the teaching of modern languages, an ancient language (most likely Latin or Ancient Greek) presents challenges with grammar that may be beyond the grasp of the generalist school teacher. Primary practitioners who deliver Latin or Ancient Greek will have to become confident in conjugating verbs and declining nouns. That said, there are undoubted benefits to studying the classics if only to give pupils an insight into life in Ancient Rome and Greece. Latin in particular can help children to appreciate the derivation of words in English and assist them with a better understanding of their spelling. An understanding of Latin and Ancient Greek can also help children to learn other languages, especially those of western Europe; this is referred to in the 'Purpose of study' section of the Languages document.

The dominance of European languages in the education system at high school implies inevitably that the Romance languages (French and Spanish) will be the most popular European languages chosen. Transition from Key Stage 2 to Key Stage 3 can be problematic; changing languages from Key Stage 2 to 3 may also be detrimental to some learners who may not acquire a new language so readily. It is essential that high schools are able to continue teaching the same languages as their feeder primaries and that there is continuity in the learning if the pupils are to benefit fully from learning languages at an earlier age. The curriculum does not apply to teaching in Key Stage 1. Although some primary schools have been teaching a foreign language before Key Stage 2, it can only be regarded as a wasted opportunity that the National Curriculum establishes languages as a foundation subject from the age of seven.

The content of the Key Stage 2 language curriculum focuses upon the development of the four key skills: listening, speaking, reading, writing. Ancient languages will not need to focus upon the oral (including pronunciation and intonation) aspects of the programme of study. The focus for language learning here is on reading, although the pupils may engage in simple oral exercises. Modern languages focus upon practical communication, employing all the four language skills. There is no prescription in the contents about methodology although the 'Programmes of study' do stress the kinds of opportunities that would promote good practice in language learning. Teachers are free to exercise their professional judgement as to how the language content is delivered. This autonomy is to be welcomed. However, teachers have to be clear about progression across the key stage and how this is measured. Funding cuts at local authority level mean that support for schools could be an issue; resourcing a new subject on the timetable will be a challenge for some schools when there is a lack of government willingness to provide guidance and practical help. The profession needs guidance to establish a national framework of progress measures that is applicable to all schools. The Common European Framework of Reference (Council of Europe 2001) could be very useful in providing such support.

Reflection points

- *Read the list of objectives for languages on pages 194–195 of the National Curriculum 2014.*
- *Consider two languages (modern or ancient) while thinking about your responses to the following questions. Which objectives are a challenge/not a challenge to you personally? Which objectives do you think are a challenge/not a challenge to teach young children?*

The pedagogy of languages

This lens explores planning for languages. The National Curriculum is focused on the development of the four language skills: speaking, listening, reading and writing (the last two only for ancient languages). Linear language teaching (progression in one language) requires careful planning that takes into account prior learning in particular since language teaching needs to be structured around previous learning experiences. Individual lesson plans will fit into units of work that focus on particular themes. Early language teaching will have a particular focus on speaking and listening, which are fundamental to learning the target language.

Learning objectives need to be very focused in language learning. 'To know and understand vocabulary items' often needs to be carefully considered as a learning objective. Think instead about the four language skills. It is always a good idea to envisage what the children will be doing in the lesson as part of the planning process; this can often assist with accuracy in the planning. Rather than knowing/understanding, the lesson objective might be 'To practise accurate pronunciation of vocabulary items' or 'To be able to spell vocabulary accurately'. Within grammar, the learning objectives need to be tightly focused; envisage what it is that the children need to learn and to do in the lesson: 'To be able to recognise masculine and feminine nouns' and 'To be able to identify patterns in the language' is more accurate than 'To know about gender in nouns'.

Planning and assessment

Language activities need to be planned with assessment in mind. The learning objectives generate the lesson opportunities; the assessment opportunities provide evidence of the extent to which the learning objectives have been achieved. If the lesson is created around a format of:

- present (what is taught)
- practise (what the children do to start to acquire the language)
- produce (what the children do to show they have acquired the language)

the assessment needs to fit into this.

The assessment of pronunciation for its accuracy (use of digital recording equipment? other adults?) will be very different from how writing in the language is assessed. A useful strategy is to introduce new vocabulary items within language structures that the children are already familiar with, or to introduce new language structures using existing vocabulary items. Language learning strategies should be identified as part of the activities when there is a need to raise awareness of these. The types of teaching activities generally fall under each of the four headings described below.

Speaking and listening activities are highly dependent upon the teacher and effective use of resources in the classroom. Most children will need frequent speaking and listening opportunities since they will not get these outside the classroom in the second language (unless the language studied is a community language). Pronunciation is entirely dependent upon the children being able to listen to a good model of pronunciation that is provided by the teacher, recorded and online songs, poems and rhymes, audio stories, video material and native speakers. The children will need time to be able to speak in the target language and to create their own spoken sentences so that they can have simple yet meaningful language exchanges. This element in the planning needs to identify differentiation in the target language to suit the needs of the learners. This might involve controlling the amount of target language to be employed by different groups within the class. The use of resources in the lesson could be closely related to the form of assessment that is used for speaking and listening.

Reading and writing activities are not separate from speaking and listening. Most lessons will incorporate elements of each language skill; speaking and listening underpin development in reading and writing, and the link is made clear when studying the relationship between sounds and the written form of the language (phoneme and grapheme correspondence). It is helpful to make comparisons with English (or their own language) when studying spelling in the target language. Word-level activities can include studying how words are borrowed from the target language or given to the target language from the first language. Bilingual dictionaries are useful for developing skills in sequencing the letters in the alphabet. Sentence-level work includes grammatical activities and use of punctuation. Text-level work would let the children read and identify the features of different types of fiction and non-fiction writing. The National Curriculum clearly specifies stories, songs, poems and rhymes in the language; however describing people, places, things and actions orally and in writing (penultimate statement in the languages document) could be achieved through the study of non-fiction texts. Differentiation could be achieved by the amount of scaffolding provided to ability groups.

Grammar activities are taught through the language skills, and focus on the function of nouns, verbs, adjectives and adverbs in particular. Making comparisons between the grammar of the first language and target language can help children to understand better how their own language operates. Different types of writing are useful for introducing grammar to children; identifying gender in nouns or tenses in verbs, for example, is usefully achieved through a shared text (a story, song, poem, etc.).

The National Curriculum points to the importance of appreciating classical civilisation if an ancient language is studied. Teaching children about the culture (both capital

'C' and small 'c') of modern-day language groups is just as important. Intercultural understanding can be carefully planned for in some language lessons to provide a useful context for language. Resources are of particular importance to this aspect of language learning. Above all the children need to be aware of stereotyping, and sensitivity in how children are exposed to cultural identity needs to feature in the planning. Role play in the language, employing the cultural features of the target language group, is a very useful means of raising awareness of aspects of the lifestyle or national identity of those speakers. Children will be able to make comparisons with their own personal and national contexts depending upon the stage of their development.

The plan can also incorporate cross-curricular links with other subjects, particularly if there is to be any teaching of another curriculum subject in the foreign language.

The overall structure of a lesson plan can adopt a starter/main activities/plenary format that practitioners are familiar with in other subjects in the curriculum. The length of time that the individual sections of the lesson last for need to be indicated on the plan. This will be dependent upon the time allocated to language teaching, but the age of the children and how much language learning they have had previously is also important in structuring a lesson that best suits their needs. The importance of establishing routines and affording lots of opportunities for repetition of language within lessons cannot be stressed too much. Assessment for Learning can appear in a variety of guises: effective questioning, mini-plenaries, feedback, peer and self-assessment. It is important in language teaching to include the target language that you wish to use not only for the content of the teaching episode but also to direct the children in the lesson. Instructions that are used to manage the children's behaviour in the target language are useful for the practitioner if recorded on the plan, and can certainly boost confidence in using the target language.

Finally, there needs to be a twofold evaluation. The first is of the lesson so that the next lesson can be planned for meaningfully by building on the children's prior knowledge. The second evaluation needs to be an honest reflection on the quality of the teaching and learning – critical self-evaluation for the purpose of professional development.

Reflection point

- *Imagine that you had to teach a lesson (or part of a lesson) on modern foreign language learning in the target language. What are the key sentences/vocabulary items that you would need to be able to employ? How would you help children to understand this language?*

The languages teacher's toolkit

Teaching languages: starting off

- Sing lots of songs. Hearing the sounds of the language early on and relating these to meaning is important.
- Establish contact with a school of target language speakers. Skype is a useful technology for this.

- Working in pairs is a particularly useful organisational strategy for language work. Pairs can be reorganised as the occasion demands it. Encourage speech about the children themselves. Bio-data is useful: name, address, age, family relationships, interests, pets, likes/dislikes. Focus on the use of first person singular, 'I', in the target language and core verbs in the language: to be, like, wish, have. Encourage the children to ask questions relating to bio-data as well as being able to respond to these questions.

- Hand puppets can easily be made from envelopes or socks that are adorned with facial features! These can then be questioned by the children, or the puppets can ask the children the questions. Each puppet can have its own set of bio-data to extend the children's use of vocabulary.

- A useful way of stimulating the children's imagination further is to use cut-out characters from magazines (particularly if they are in colour) or newspapers; celebrities from the world of sport, TV and music are obvious choices. Let the children bring in their own selection. They can then imagine how their character(s) would express ideas, likes and wishes, and create a sentence or sentences using first person singular contained within a speech bubble.

Speaking and listening

Discriminating sounds

National Curriculum objective: explore the patterns and sounds of language through songs and rhymes, and link the spelling, sound and meanings of words.

Using songs and rhymes is a very useful vehicle for practising phonic awareness. Use specific sounds in the song/rhyme to focus on to practise awareness of sounds that are based on one letter or combination of letters. For example, the children have to raise their hand every time they hear the 'd' sound when they sing 'Sur le pont d'Avignon'. This is easy to extend to other words chosen by the teacher that the children respond to each time they hear the 'd' sound. This is best done on a regular basis. The same song can be sung and a different sound chosen each time. This is especially important for those sounds that exist in the target language that English does not have; children will need lots of practice listening to these sounds so that they can repeat them accurately.

Role play with paintings

National Curriculum objective: engage in conversations; ask and answer questions.
National Curriculum objective: speak in sentences, using familiar vocabulary, phrases and basic language structures.

Role play is an excellent strategy for developing language and practising existing language structures and vocabulary. An interesting way of developing characterisation is through the use of paintings that depict scenes from everyday life. Searching for such images is made easy through Google. Paintings of street scenes, busy stations, cafe and restaurant images can provide a very useful context within which to structure learning. Carefully chosen works of art can also provide an intercultural understanding opportunity that can be exploited through cross-curricular links. Auguste Renoir's paintings 'Dance at Le Moulin de La Galette' and 'The Luncheon of the Boating Party' provide opportunities for asking factual questions about the scenes that probe factual understanding:

- 'Combien de filles voyez-vous?'
- 'Il y a combien de bouteilles sur la table?'
- 'Est-ce qu'il ya un chat ou un chien?'

Ask questions that require an imaginative response:

- 'Comment s'appelle la jeune fille aux cheveux blonds?'
- 'Qu'est-ce qu'elle boit, la dame?'

Interrogating the painting can then lead to the children assuming the identity of one of the characters. Start with the children, one group at a time, assuming the frozen pose of the character they have adopted. Each time the children speak, they come out of the frozen position and behave naturally. When their language exchange has finished, they resume their frozen pose as in the painting. The children can respond to questions about bio-data from the audience and ask questions of the other characters in the scene that they interact with in the painting.

Reading and writing

Dictionary work

National Curriculum objective: broaden their vocabulary and develop their ability to understand new words that are introduced into familiar written material, including through using a dictionary.

This work builds upon children's skills in using dictionaries in English. Skills in being able to use a bilingual dictionary develop as literacy skills develop. Putting familiar items of vocabulary (e.g. clothes, family members) into alphabetical order can start this work off without even using a dictionary. This can be easily developed by choosing a selection of words that start with the same letter in the target language; the children have to apply the order of the alphabet to the second letter to identify how to sequence the words alphabetically, e.g. sehr, Schwimmbad, Stunde, sagen. In alphabetical order the sequence is: sagen, Schwimmbad, sehr, Stunde. Check the order in a dictionary and find the words' meanings. Use the words in sentences, building upon children's existing language structures.

Practise working through the alphabet in the sounds of the letter in the target language.

Identify and write down the first words under chosen letters, e.g. d, s, l. Identify the last word under the same letters. Now identify the fourth word, and so on.

What is the first word with am, en, ha, etc.?

Use dictionaries to identify the first/last noun, verb, adjective under different letters.

Give the children a list of target vocabulary. Practise pronunciation of the words. Children to identify the meaning of the words and record in their own bilingual vocabulary books.

Creating loop games

National Curriculum objective: describe people, places, things and actions orally and in writing.

A loop game can be introduced to the children early on in language learning. When they are familiar with the structure they can create questions and answers about themselves or

Table 7.1 Table loop game

START	Je m'appelle Sophie	J'ai dix ans
Comment t'appelles-tu?	Quel âge-as tu?	Quelle es ta couleur
END		préférée?
J'ai un chien		
Rouge	**J'ai un frère et une soeur**	**J'aime jouer du piano**
Est-ce que tu as des frères ou des soeurs?	Qu'est-ce que tu aimes faire?	Est-ce que tu as des animaux domestiques?

the lives of people they know (about). The teacher models the loop game initially to the children. When the children write their own loop games, the questions can be supplied by the teacher. Later the children may choose from a list of questions. Finally the children may suggest their own questions when they have become more confident in using the language.

An example of a loop game for a group of six children is presented in Table 7.1.

Grammar

Identifying parts of speech
National Curriculum objective: understand basic grammar appropriate to the language being studied, including (where relevant) feminine, masculine and neuter forms and the conjugation of high-frequency verbs … how to apply these, to build sentences, and how these differ from or are similar to English.

Use actions to denote parts of speech. This is a very kinaesthetic approach to teaching grammar that is fun and effective in helping children to identify the different types of words that exist in both spoken and written language. The activity will help to develop children's ability to analyse sentence structure. Direct comparisons with English need to be made to help the children to understand how grammar operates in similar and different ways across languages. It is always best to build up this knowledge incrementally. Model sentences regularly so that the children become aware of the function of words in sentences.

- Noun: both hands on head
- Verb: walk on the spot (if the children are seated on a carpet or at their desks while doing this work the action can be performed by children using two fingers as legs walking on the carpet/desk)
- Pronoun: one hand on the head (since the pronoun replaces a noun in a sentence, the action has to be similar to that for noun)
- Adjective: wave one hand next to the head (this takes place in the same vicinity as the actions for noun and pronoun since adjectives describe these two parts of speech)
- Adverb: brisk movement of arms as if walking quickly (the exaggerated movement tells us more about the action, which is the function of adverbs)
- Conjunction: the left hand shakes hands with the right hand (and/but are conjunctions; conjunctions join clauses and sentences together)
- Prepositions: point with a finger (typically words that denote position, such as in, on, through, under; with is also a preposition)

Organise the children to discuss in pairs sentences that they read/hear or that they create themselves (written/spoken). The level of challenge depends upon their familiarity with and understanding of parts of speech.

- Servus laborat (the slave is working)
  (both hands on head) (walk on the spot)
- El perro está en la calle (the dog is in the street)
  (both hands on head) (walk on the spot) (point with finger) (both hands on head)
- Je chante fort dans la salle de bains (I sing loudly in the bathroom)
  (one hand by head) (brisk movement of arms as if walking quickly) (point with finger) (both hands on head)

Understanding adjectival agreement

Learning objective: understand basic grammar appropriate to the language being studied, including (where relevant) feminine, masculine and neuter forms and how to apply these, to build sentences, and how these differ from or are similar to English.

Build up a bank of nouns and adjectives related to a topic. Use flash cards to teach the nouns and adjectives. Masculine nouns need to be on one colour of card with a picture and the definite and indefinite article; feminine nouns on a different colour; neuter nouns (if applicable) on a third colour. These need to be on display and highly visible. Have a second bank of words on display showing the masculine, feminine, neuter forms of adjectives, each form of the adjective being on the same colour of card. When the children make a sentence using the cards in front of the class they will have the noun and the adjective next to each other on the same colour of card to denote adjectival agreement with the noun. For example, in a topic on clothes, all masculine nouns might be on orange card (le/un pantalon, le/un T-shirt, le/un jean); all feminine nouns on green card (la/une jupe, la/une cravate, la/une veste). The children might also practise colours that they have been taught previously. Masculine forms of adjectives of colour would each be written on orange card (noir, bleu, blanc, rouge …), feminine forms on green card (noire, bleue, blanche, rouge …). The children might say and act out I wear (je porte) or I put on (je mets) and then hold up the card showing the article of clothing followed by the adjective on the matching colour of card, e.g. Je mets un pantalon (orange card) noir (orange card). Discuss with the children the importance of word order (French and Spanish most often have adjectives after the nouns) and compare with English. The children can transfer this learning into their own writing by using the same colours of pencils (here orange and green) when writing their own sentences with nouns and adjectives.

Reflection point

- *Think about the rest of the primary curriculum that you work with. How might you use the foreign language to deliver some aspects of other curriculum subjects to the children? Which specific items of vocabulary that the children have already encountered can you practise in this way?*

Summary of key points

- Foreign languages at Key Stage 2 are the most recent area of the curriculum to attain foundation subject status.
- The importance of learning a language from an early age reflects the role of languages in a world where communication between language groups is facilitated by cheaper and faster means of travel and by the use of IT.
- Foreign languages at Key Stage 2 have been introduced into primary schools throughout the first decade of the twenty-first century, although there has not been any uniform strategy to assist this development.
- Real issues remain about the ability of primary school teachers to be able to deliver foreign languages competently.
- Choice of language should not be considered out of context. This depends as much on neighbouring primary schools and the main receiving high school.
- Ancient languages may be taught at Key Stage 2 though they will not be continued in Key Stage 3.
- The National Curriculum focuses on the acquisition of the four language skills and on developing an understanding of and competence in grammar; intercultural understanding, although important, does not have any prominence in the documentation.
- Speaking and listening, reading and writing need to be taught in interactive and fun ways; there is no guidance referring to methodology.
- Progression and continuity need to be planned for carefully to ensure that children make 'substantial progress in one language', although 'substantial progress' is not defined.
- There is a need for guidance concerning assessment.
- Careful planning is required to secure learning supported by appropriate resources.
- Foreign languages are able to provide the medium for the delivery of (parts of) other subjects; exploit such cross-curricular links wherever possible.
- There are many toolkit ideas to teach foreign languages. Children need to practise the four skills regularly to aid language acquisition.

References

Byram, M. and Doyé, P. (1999) Intercultural competence and foreign language learning in the primary school. In Driscoll, P. and Frost, D. (eds) *The Teaching of Modern Languages in the Primary School.* London: Routledge.

CfBT Education Trust (2014) Language trends 2013/14: the state of language learning in primary and secondary schools in England. Online at: www.cfbt.com/en-GB/Research/Research-library/2014/r-language-trends-2014 (accessed August 2014).

Council of Europe (2001) *Common European Framework of Reference for Languages: Learning, Teaching, Assessment.* Cambridge: Cambridge University Press. Online at: www.coe.int/t/dg4/linguistic/cadre1_en.asp (accessed August 2014).

Coyle, D., Hood, P. and Marsh, D. (2010) *Content and Language Integrated Learning.* Cambridge: Cambridge University Press.

Dearing, R. and King, L. (2007) *Languages Review.* Nottingham: DfES Publications. Online at: http://webarchive.nationalarchives.gov.uk/20130401151715/http://www.education.gov.uk/publications/standard/publicationDetail/Page1/DFES-00212–2007 (accessed August 2014).

Department for Education (DfE) (2013) *The National Curriculum for England Framework Document.* London: DfE.

DfES (2002) *Languages for All: Languages for Life: A Strategy for England.* London: DfES.

DfES (2005) *The Key Stage 2 Framework for Languages.* London: DfES. Online at: http://webarchive.nationalarchives.gov.uk/20130401151715/http://www.education.gov.uk/publications/standard/publicationDetail/Page1/DFES%201721%202005 (accessed August 2014).

Driscoll, P. and Frost, D. (1999) *The Teaching of Modern Foreign Languages in the Primary School.* London: Routledge.

Jones, J. and Coffey, I. (2006) *Modern Foreign Languages 5–11. A Guide for Teachers.* London: David Fulton.

Nuffield Foundation (2000) *Languages: The Next Generation.* London: Nuffield Foundation. Online at: www.nuffieldfoundation.org/sites/default/files/languages_finalreport.pdf (accessed August 2014).

Qualifications and Curriculum Authority (QCA) (2007) *A Scheme of Work for Key Stage 2 French.* QCA/07/3087. London: QCA. Online at: http://webarchive.nationalarchives.gov.uk/20090608182316/http://standards.dfes.gov.uk/schemes3/subjects/primary_mff/?view=get (accessed August 2014).

8 Music

Ian Shirley

The late evening train from Liverpool was crowded and full of noise already, when a rather flushed-looking man, unsteady on his feet, stood up and addressed a song to the whole carriage. Soon, the singing erupted and everyone in the carriage joined in. Traditional songs, pop songs, hits by the Beatles: everyone seemed to know the words, and everyone seemed happy to be singing along.

On another night, a choir gather in a classroom for a pre-concert warm-up. Lots of nerves and excitement. The event is important: it is the culmination of everything they have been working on over the term. People gather up their folders and arrange themselves into line, ready to walk on to the stage. From the moment they enter the hall, they are no longer a group of individuals. They become one body, singing with one voice. Working together as a single instrument.

In the school classroom, the children are full of high spirits. They are about to perform their Christmas play. Costumes are ready, words are learned and this is the moment they have been waiting for. Mums and dads, nans and grandads have gathered in the hall. The teacher gathers the children together and calls for silence, ready to walk to the hall. As they assemble in front of the audience cameras flash and waves are exchanged between children and parents. These are the most special times in school, and ones that both parents and children tend to remember for ever!

In my garden, my six year old runs across the grass with a white blanket flowing out behind her. 'Is it flowing?' she asks, as she relives a moment from her most favourite Disney film. Bursting into a chorus of 'Let it go' her singing is loud enough to entertain all of our neighbours. For that moment, she is Elsa!

Music is a common characteristic of all human societies. It bridges the gap between the intellectual world, the sensory world and the world of feeling. It is at one with dance, and is as elemental as breathing; as the beat of the heart; as the cry of a baby. The National Curriculum (DfEE 1999: 122) stated, 'Music is a powerful, unique form of communication that can change the way pupils feel, think and act.' In this chapter, I will consider what it is about music that is so important to all human lives, what good practice in music teaching might be, and ideas that you may try on placement, to get a feel for teaching music and for supporting musical development.

The identity of music

At the start of this chapter I began to explore how different people make music in different ways. Yet the real world of music is much more varied than this. Children in school, teenagers in bedrooms and garages, a samba band in a city centre, a young singer at an open-mike night in a local club, a father singing to his baby in the bath. Music is a fundamental part of most human lives. It is representative of our culture and the people we want to be associated with. Our society, and the music market, has helped us to become expert listeners and consumers of music. Through education we should help children become performers, composers and directors of music, and help them to develop a broad view and an open mind to all musical forms.

So often we are persuaded by economic justifications within education – getting a good job, producing future workers. Education is about a good job – but it is also about a good life! Children have a right to a rich and happy childhood, and curriculum music is just one aspect of that rich experience. Humans engage with music because it both satisfies our intellectual curiosity and it provides a means of exploring our capacity to be expressive. Music is a puzzle that requires rehearsal, practice; working and re-working; listening and re-listening. No two musical performances are the same, and performers and composers spend their lives developing new ideas within the performance, interpretation and composition of music.

Since its introduction into general education, music has served a variety of purposes and ideologies: to promote singing in church, to enhance the experience of childhood, to protect the musical heritage, to enhance cultural taste, to promote economic prosperity. Each of these ideas holds some merit, and it is worth keeping an open mind with regard to the values of the subject about what you think. Sadly, many trainees report limited opportunity to observe curriculum music teaching, or to teach the subject themselves. Increasingly, trainees are able to observe whole-class instrumental teaching and singing, but curriculum music is less apparent. What is clear is that teacher-led instrumental work and singing (performance) has become a more dominant feature of music education, and child-led creative activities of composing, improvising and directing music are less obvious.

Reflection points

- *Investigate wider opportunities through an internet search.*
- *Find out about your local music education hub/music service.*
- *Try to find out how schools use these services.*

The music curriculum

The introduction of the first National Curriculum for music in England was certainly not a smooth process. A fundamental difference in opinion emerged between the music working party, right-wing intellectuals and the secretary of state, Kenneth Clarke. For the music working party, music education was to be a largely practical and experiential subject. They believed all children had the capacity to make music, and to make progress in music, and that there should be a broad curriculum of four attainment targets: performing, composing, listening and appraising. Right-wing politicians were more concerned for the preservation of the musical heritage, and of passing on to children a knowledge about the lives and works of great composers. This fundamental difference is indicative of the many differences that exist within music education still, and you should notice these in your wider reading.

Provision in music is complex. Local authority music services, music education charities, orchestras, choirs, music schools, universities and private individuals complement school provision in some way. In some circumstances provision is tailored to match the needs of the local community. In others, provision has been a little more limited. In some schools, teachers teach their own music, while in others music is taught by a visiting teacher, or additional member of staff, who comes into the class once a week. The best option, I suspect, is for the class teacher and the visiting teacher to work together.

The underlying structure of the most recent National Curriculum for music is founded on a set of programmes of study that have become well established in music education in the UK: performing, composing, listening and appraising. In addition, the most recent curriculum places equal emphasis on reading musical notation and on developing an understanding of music history. The National Curriculum proposes the development of musical skills and knowledge through a rich and broad musical experience. The guidance is very brief, but it does describe the key aims of music, and progression between Key Stage 1 and Key Stage 2, in the way described in the following section.

The aims of music in the National Curriculum

The aims of the National Curriculum are described in the following three statements (DfE 2013: 231).

The National Curriculum for music aims to ensure that all pupils:

- perform, listen to, review and evaluate music across a range of historical periods, genres, styles and traditions, including the works of the great composers and musicians
- learn to sing and to use their voices, to create and compose music on their own and with others, have the opportunity to learn a musical instrument, use technology appropriately and have the opportunity to progress to the next level of musical excellence
- understand and explore how music is created, produced and communicated, including through the inter-related dimensions – pitch, duration, dynamics, tempo, timbre, texture, structure and appropriate musical notations.

Curriculum content

The National Curriculum recognises that the voice provides a unique and personal resource for all children in their music learning. Furthermore, it recognises that vocal work isn't just about singing, but is also about developing rhythmic awareness and creative musical invention. In Key Stage 1, children 'use their voices expressively and creatively by singing songs and speaking chants and rhymes.' In Key Stage 2, children continue to sing, but with 'increasing confidence and control'. As children develop their singing they gain control over their ability to sing accurately in pitch, in rhythm and with a sense of style. Welch (1986) has written about the process of development in children's singing.

The National Curriculum recognises that music is also about the development of instrumental skills and that, in Key Stage 1, children should 'play tuned and untuned instruments musically'. The emphasis here is on the development of control and expression, as children get to know, through repeated engagement, what a variety of instruments can do. In Key Stage 2, children learn to play instruments 'with increasing accuracy, fluency, control and expression'. Again, the emphasis here is on the development of skill, but don't assume this comes about through formal direct teaching. Children develop their instrumental capacity through playing, performing, composing, improvising, experimenting and exploring.

Creative experimentation isn't just the means by which children learn to gain control over their instrument. Composing and improvising are important ways through which children become 'musical'. In Key Stage 1, children 'experiment with, create, select and combine sounds using the inter-related dimensions of music'. They gain confidence in playing with musical ideas – making up musical sounds for parts of a story, or creating a piece of music for a snow dance. They develop their 'feelingfulness' for music through dancing and creative play with instruments on a sound table. In Key Stage 2, children 'develop an understanding of musical composition, organising and manipulating ideas within musical structures and reproducing sounds from aural memory'. There is increasing formality here, but always opportunities to explore and form ideas. The National Curriculum adds, children should 'improvise and compose music for a range of purposes'.

Just as with art, teachers need to encourage playful experimentation in children's music making. The pallet in music education includes voices, tuned and untuned percussion, body percussion and voices. And in each of these the 'inter-related dimensions' of pitch, duration, dynamics, tempo, timbre, texture, structure, silence, rhythm are the means by which the children can explore and experiment with this pallet.

Throughout children's music education they should listen to music from a wide range of styles and genres. Focused listening should help children explore the infinite possibilities music presents, and it should help them see how other composers have dealt with musical ideas. In Key Stage 1, children 'listen with concentration and understanding to a range of high-quality live and recorded music'. In Key Stage 2, they 'listen with attention to detail and recall sounds with increasing aural memory', having access to the best music from all around the world. Notice how the focus of their listening becomes more formal and focused, matching the developing formality in their use of musical structures in their composition and improvisatory work; however, music listening should never be a chore, and should be designed with the needs of individual groups of children in mind.

> ### Reflection points
>
> - *Read through these aims, and list all the things there are to learn about in music. Consider which aspects of music you might be able to support in your classroom, and for which aspects you would need to draw on the services of visiting primary music specialists. Try to notice how this changes as you gain experience of working with children.*
> - *Consider the following questions: What do you feel is the most important aspect of music in school? What music/musicians would you like to introduce children to? Should the class teacher teach their own music lessons? What do you want your pupils to get from music?*

The pedagogy of music

In its 2012 report on music education, Ofsted suggested that there were seven priorities. Some of these are related to school management and are not relevant to the discussion in this chapter. Others concern teaching and learning, and these have informed the discussion that follows in this section.

Teaching music musically: music as the dominant discourse of the classroom

David Elliot, an influential American philosopher on music education, claims that, essentially, music is an 'intentional human practice' (2005: 30). It isn't simply a matter of organising sound – a pneumatic drill has an organised sound! Nor is music a universal language; music has cultural relevance that can only be understood through cultural immersion. Chinese music, for example, or opera, or certain forms of pop music, may mean absolutely nothing to some people, but will be loved by others. What is universal is that music has the potential to affect human emotions. Universally, human beings engage with music, music serves the same purposes of celebration, meditation, dance, play and, as Elliot goes on to suggest, all music consists of four dimensions: music makers (musicers); musical activity (musicing); a product (music); and a context (such as musical genre, style or event).

The best music teaching engages children in the real world of music. School music should not be distinct from the outside world, but part of it. Keith Swanwick (1999: 108), one of the most influential writers on music in the curriculum, argues that schools that value music promote musical discourses. What is more, he argues that children only become musicians by being musicians, engaging in musical practices and interacting with other musicians in musical discourse. The best teaching is that which nurtures the children as real musicians, what Wenger (1998) calls a community of practice. It is frugal with spoken language, and promotes learning through musical repetition and modelling. 'Musical' music teaching promotes the practices of real musicians – it focuses on difficult passages, breaks musical passages down for slow rehearsal, it seeks opportunities to share and try out ideas in progress. Finally, it seeks the opportunity for musical performance. Musical teaching values technology as a means to record, store and review work in progress.

Sound before symbol

When I started to learn to play a brass instrument in the local town band, the first session was spent learning the note middle C. I was shown middle C on the paper and shown how to play it on my instrument. There was a tacit view that reading notation and instrumental learning went hand in hand.

Consider for a moment how you learn to read. Before you could read you could already speak. Furthermore, you could listen and understand what others were saying, too. You improvised sentences and you engaged in conversations with others. Musical notation, and there are many forms, is a really important part of musical learning, but the formality of crotchets and quavers should be introduced only after children have had lots of experience of making music. Through composing and improvising with instruments, singing, making up rhythms, moving and dancing, listening to all sorts of music, and improvising music with other people, children steadily 'come to know' music. They come to accept certain conventions, such as 'higher and lower' or 'louder and quieter'. In the early years children march to music, they make big and small shapes in response to music, and they use pieces of fabric to twirl and dance with the snow-flake music. This is really important as it begins to establish the connection between sound, symbol and gesture.

Improve pupils' internalisation of music through high-quality singing and listening

Singing

There are some simple principles of good song teaching that will help you to make good progress with your classes, to teach songs efficiently, to create individual interpretations and to improve the quality of singing in your class. To begin, you need to make sure you really know the song you want to teach. There is a difference between teaching it effectively and teaching it correctly, and it is hard to correct mistakes once they have been rehearsed.

Decide on how you will set about teaching the song. Here are some principles.

- Sing the song all the way through – one verse and the chorus will be enough for long songs, to begin. Demonstrate what it is the children will be learning.
- Try to teach without talking, using lots of modelling and repetition. You sing a phrase (we call this 'chunking') to the children – they sing it back.
- Do this all the way through.
- Now, without losing the flow of the rehearsal, join together some of the phrases or chunks. Do this to the end.
- If there is a section that isn't quite right, don't stop to talk about it, just model it again, emphasising how it should sound.
- For younger children, gestures can really help them to remember the words and to emphasise key aspects of expression. Guide them with such movements, but also invite them to think about gestures that could be used
- Now you might want to sing the song all the way through again, allowing the children to listen.
- When you are ready get the children to sing all the way through. Now it is your job to stop singing and to listen!

I would try to do all this without stopping. Keep the rehearsal flowing, and the lesson will be efficient and musical. The class will make really quick progress, and the quality of singing should be very good.

Assessment in singing

Always be clear what you are trying to achieve in your teaching; this will help you to assess the quality of children's teaching. Children should have the chance to listen to the quality of their singing. Try to record their performances and get them to appraise the results. Invite them to make suggestions about interpretations: dynamics, different groups singing certain lines, etc. Get them to be imaginative in their singing, so that the performances are really exciting.

Ask them to listen out for:

- accuracy
- diction
- variations in dynamics
- a sense of togetherness (what might be called 'ensemble' or 'choral blend')
- beginning and ending together
- expression.

It is often useful to discuss the performances of others as they are working on their own performances, so they feel part of a wider community of musicians. The idea of 'school music' can sometimes limit children's expectations of what can be achieved in school.

Planning for music

The New Labour government under Tony Blair and Gordon Brown brought a period of intense government intervention in the micro-practices of schools. One intervention concerned the publication of a series of schemes of work, published by the QCA (still available at: http://webarchive.nationalarchives.gov.uk/20100612050234/http:/www.standards.dfes.gov.uk/schemes3/subjects/?view=get).

These schemes attempted to show progression through certain key musical concepts and were part of a 'standards' agenda (Stunnell 2006), however they were misinterpreted and adopted by schools as complete schemes of work. In 2010 the Coalition government came to power in the UK and, while many of the New Labour initiatives, such as the Standards Site schemes of work, have been withdrawn, the emphasis on standards, knowledge and achievement remains high. In the next section I will discuss what musical progression might be.

Musical progression through and across the curriculum

There are a number of things you need to find out before you begin planning for music. Does the school have an existing scheme of work? What planning is already in place? Who currently teaches music? Where and when does music teaching take place? What experiences have the children already had, both in terms of classroom music teaching, whole-class instrumental teaching, singing opportunities, performance opportunities, listening opportunities and creative opportunities? What knowledge, skills and understanding have the children already acquired? What does their class teacher think they need to develop? Some of these questions may be addressed to other teachers; some might be addressed to the children; and some might require careful listening and observation.

A medium-term plan should provide for a rounded music education. In all aspects of music education children should continue to develop their ability to sing, to play instruments, to compose, to gain understanding of musical form and style, to learn more about the relationship between musical sounds and symbolic representation, and to appraise their achievement and musical output. Your medium-term plan will do two things.

1. It should set out the kinds of activities you intend to undertake during the period. It may explain songs, games, musical styles, and opportunities for compositions and performance.
2. It must indicate the kind of progression children will be making during the period in all aspects of music curriculum. This is really important, and you should know, before you decide on the activities they will undertake, what it is you want the children to learn.

A good starting point for deciding on what you want the children to learn (and what you will assess) is presented in the ISME framework, available at: http://www.ism.org/news/ article/ism-publishes-assessment-and-progression-framework. This framework is written by Martin Faultley and Alison Daubney, who have both contributed much to discussions about assessment in music.

Each lesson will probably have a number of elements: warm-ups, singing activities, composing tasks and focusing activities, which involve listening and discussion. There should be time for exploration and forming of ideas, and regular opportunities for sharing work in progress.

The importance of planning

The thinking that goes into your short-term planning is more important than the template or document you complete for your teaching file. Planning is thinking, and involves carefully matching a group of children with a set of learning objectives and a set of learning activities. Each of these three things is equally important!

Once you have identified the learning focus for the lesson, you can decide on the kinds of activities you would like the children to do. You could choose these from those set out above or a published book. You'll need to think about:

- what is the learning focus
- how you will introduce the ideas
- how the lesson will begin, develop and end
- how you will teach any songs
- how you will organise the space
- how you will give out the instruments
- how you will use other adults, and how you will attend to different children's learning needs
- how you will manage time – for example, setting the children timed goals
- where you will provide opportunities to share work in progress and give the children a chance to appraise their work

- who you will assess – you should focus your assessment, in any lesson, around a particular group of children; however, you should note any significant developments in all children's music making
- what you will assess – this should relate directly to your learning objectives
- how you will assess – informally, as they are working; formally, in a final performance; through observation; through questioning; teacher assessment; peer assessment; or self-assessment – each should play a part in your assessment plan.

A note about differentiation

You should not assume that children's potential in music is related to their achievement in core subjects. Music is verbal, it doesn't involve spelling or reading words, and it provides a new set of challenges that can stimulate the engagement of all children.

Music as a process: use technology to promote creativity, widen inclusion and make assessment more musical

Composing is a really tricky word and scares many teachers. I prefer to call it 'making up stuff'. Composing is what you do when you whistle a made-up tune or tap a rhythm with a pencil. It isn't a musical free-for-all, and as I will show later, it involves creative play with important musical structures.

All creative arts operate through a similar process, though using fundamentally different concepts, materials and forms. The process isn't linear but includes the opportunity to explore new ideas, techniques and skills, before beginning to form these into some kind of product. Once formed the product can be tested out on a small number of people, as work in progress, and, through feedback and appraisal, the work undergoes further change and development, before being submitted to final performance or exhibition. After this, the artist reflects on her or his work, and considers possibilities for their future work. This is called the 'process of the arts'.

This process of exploring, forming, presenting work in progress, re-forming, performing and evaluating, is common to all forms of art, and is helpful in all aspects of music making. It is a very useful structure on which to base a unit of work. This is a useful process in the context of school, because it reminds you that art making is not a straightforward process. Furthermore, it suggests all creative work involves the application of knowledge and skills, and the opportunity for exploring, forming and re-forming ideas.

Technology can make a significant contribution to children's creative musical activity. It provides an instant resource to record and play back music, and should be a central component of every music lesson. Technology provides for adaptation, so that more children can participate in music making. Technology allows musicians to generate musical sounds, to combine them, to sequence them, to layer them, to reverse them and to enhance them. You can't do all this at once, but even simple programes like 'Audacity' allow you to record music, and to cut, duplicate, splice, reverse and enhance recorded sounds. In addition you could use programs like Microsoft's 'Photo-story' to create multimedia presentations, to which you can then draw in the digital recording from Audacity. New software and hardware solutions are constantly being developed to support children's listening, notation reading, performance, composing and general musical understanding. Some useful resources are listed at the end of this chapter.

> **Reflection points**
>
> - *Spend some time looking at Sing Up (www.singup.org), and at other resources in libraries and school cupboards. Songbooks mostly have CDs these days, or online support materials. Begin to draw up a list of songs you would like to sing with your classes.*
> - *Download the framework, and look at the examples of learning statements listed on pages 6–7. They are examples, and you shouldn't try to see progression across the page. They are useful, however, as they indicate what you might be focusing on at four different stages of the primary phase.*
> - *The framework will help you to focus the assessment of your lessons. There should be a direct connection between your learning objectives and your assessment criteria.*

The music teachers' toolkit

In this section I have suggested a number of ideas to support your music making. To begin, just try out some of the ideas. Then, as you gain in confidence, you can begin to plan more detailed lessons, and even a series of lessons. Remember, the point is to get children making music.

Games

Passing games
Passing games are a really good way to focus children's attention, and to rehearse skills such as turn taking, listening and improvisation. Try to vary the games so the children explore the interrelated dimensions of music, too. It is usually best to play these games in a circle.

Pass the sound
The children sit in a circle. Pass a sound around the room: hand sounds, body percussion, vocalised sound. Play with each of these ideas, making sure the children are listening, watching and responding to your silent gestures. Allow the children to lead the game and use lots of smiles to reward their interaction.

Introduce rhythms: echo clapping
Let the children continue to explore sounds, but begin to introduce rhythms too. Use words to help them learn the rhythm, like this:

Co- ffee,   co- ffee,   co- ffee,   tea

Give them lots of practice, and use words relating to wider classroom themes:

Bat- man,   Bat- man,   Super- man,   Ro- bin

The trick is to make sure there is a steady beat.

Here is an extended piece for echo clapping:

| Co- ffee | co- ffee | co- ffee | tea |
| Co-ca co-la | co-ca co-la | co-ffee | tea |

Pass the rhythm

Continue to play echo games, giving children the opportunity to lead the games once the idea is established. This requires them to hear the rhythm in their heads, and to improvise. Begin to play rhythm-passing games:

| Co- ffee | co- ffee | co- ffee | tea |

Make sure they are all ready for their turn, and that they are listening and appraising as the pattern goes around the circle.

Each child plays the rhythm once, and immediately it passes to the next:

| Bat- man | Bat- man | Super- man | Run |

Once the first rhythm has started its journey around the circle, add a second rhythm that complements the first.

| Bat- man | Bat- man | Super- man | Run |
| Spi- der- man | Spi- der- man | | |

Once the game is secure, you could use gesture to indicate getting louder and quieter (not faster). See if you can turn it into a musical rhythmic performance! If it is appropriate, invite various children to lead the game. You could also transfer the rhythms to handheld percussion instruments.

Creative activities

Music allows human beings to be creative in many different ways: creative listeners, who compile imaginative playlists, and who seek new experiences, and a wide range of styles and settings, might be described as creative listeners; performers might be creative in their interpretation and delivery of existing songs and musical pieces; composers are creative in that they generate new music, often from very small musical ideas; musical directors are creative in the way they guide their singers/players, and in the way they interpret the music being performed.

In the following section I have included some ideas for creative music activity in the classroom.

Stage one: handheld percussion instruments

Rhythm is an essential element of music. Playing with rhythm offers a really important way to begin to explore making up music. Give each child a handheld percussion instrument. Give them time to explore their instruments. Invite them to make a really exciting piece that has a beginning and an end. It may be helpful to model such a piece for them.

Give each child a handheld percussion instrument, such as a wood block, a pair of claves, a bell tree, a drum or a slit drum. Allow the children time to play with the instrument. Get them to improvise a rhythmic phrase, and explore dynamic changes, silences, patterns and repetitions. Explore ideas, then share them together.

Stage two: duets, trios and musical conversations

Invite the children to work in pairs now, to create a musical conversation between their two instruments. You could model this for them with another adult. They could think about:

- question and answer (a conversation between the two instruments)
- imitation
- swapping rhythm patterns between instruments
- playing at the same time
- playing at differing dynamics (loud/quiet)
- how they will start/finish
- could one/both of the instruments have a solo moment?

Again, their final piece will be another improvisation, but they should have the chance to perform.

Assessment

The children need the opportunity to listen to and watch their performance, using modern technologies. Help them to make observations about the following:

- the quality of their ideas
- the sense of ensemble (togetherness)
- transition sections (into the start/from one section to another)
- variation in terms of sounds, rhythms or dynamics
- ideas of what they might like to do next.

Stage three: composing with words

First, you need some raw material – a rhythmic phrase: items of food, countries in the World Cup, characters in a story. The children should decide on one each and have the chance to play with them. You might get to this point over the course of one or two lessons.

Begin the third session by revising what they have done so far. Introduce the idea, now, of parts working together (layers/texture) in pairs or threes. In this session the children will improvise a duet or a trio, using their rhythmic phrases. First, they'll need to see that they can all say their rhythm patterns at the same time – you just need to make sure there is a firm pulse:

1	2	3	4
Little	Red	Rid- ing	hood

The first person repeats their line until the second person joins in or takes over:

Big	bad	wolf

These rhythms work over the top of each other, and the children can begin to improvise their composition. Get them to think about:

- starting sequence
- end sequence
- how many sections, and how the sections could differ
- embellishments to the rhythm patterns or dynamics
- how the layers will build up
- could some instruments just use a fraction of a different rhythm
- could there be any movement or drama in the performance?

Extension ideas
You could try transferring these rhythmic pieces on to handheld percussion. This creates samba music. Show the children some samba music and ask them to notice how the rhythmic phrases are repeated.

Assessment
There are two key aspects to assessment that you should note here.

First, assessment should be ongoing. As the children are working, take time to watch them and notice things about their interactions – how ideas emerge, leadership qualities, rhythmic awareness, ability to explore ideas. Second, the final performance provides you with an opportunity to collect evidence of progress and capability. Use modern technologies to record the children's work. Invite them and the group to comment on:

- their performance
- quality of ensemble
- rhythmic accuracy
- the development of ideas
- ideas for future work
- reflection on how their musical work is developing
- their understanding of ostinatos (repeated rhythmic phrases) within the composition.

Use this formal opportunity to notice and record key aspects of their music making.

Stage four: composing with melody
The work we have done so far allows you to tailor your musical work around any number of themes. It also provides you with a powerful means of getting children to explore and create musical sounds. In this section, I'm going to show you how to build on the patterns by adding melody.

Modes
Different rhythmic instruments playing together create interesting sounds because of their differing timbre (sound quality), pitch and resonance. We can extend this by focusing more closely on variation in pitch. Even two notes are enough to create a melody – think of 'Rain, rain, go away', for example.

Normal musical scales have eight notes, and are arranged over an octave, for example c, d, e, f, g, a, b, c. Other scales are also arranged over eight notes, but some of them

are a little more complex because they involve what are known as flats and sharps –
often, these use the black notes on a piano keyboard. Modes are special scales that have
been used for hundreds of years. They often have a moody, medieval or even oriental feel,
and they can be created by playing eight-note scales on any series of white notes, such as
A–A (ABCDEFGA), or D–D (DEFGABCD). Lots of folk tunes are based on modes, as are
gospel songs from America.

Listen to songs like 'Billy Jean' (Michael Jackson), 'Norwegian Wood' (The Beatles),
'Moon Dance' (Van Morrison), or folk songs such as 'She Moved Through the Fair' or
'Scarborough Fair'. These each draw on two different modes (Mixolydian and Dorian) to
create a very moody feel.

Modal composition
Begin by asking a child to play a drone, just using the home note of a mode – perhaps A.
They could add another note, a fifth above, so that they play both A and E. This is a drone.
It could go on throughout the piece. Eventually, children will find that shifting one of the
beaters, up or down, just one note, makes a huge difference to the feel of the piece.

Next invite a child to improvise a short repeating pattern that fits nicely with the
drone. Limit them to the first five notes, to begin (ABCDE). The drone and the ostinato will
provide a musical basis for improvising melodies.

Give a third child a tuned instrument, such as a glockenspiel. Limit the child, to begin,
to perhaps the first three notes of the mode (ABC). Limiting the number of notes in this
way helps the child to develop her/his inner hearing of the music she/he is about to play.
Ask them to make up a tune on these three notes that fit with the drone and the ostinato.

Once the idea is understood, children can improvise and compose music using any
combination of instruments, voices, drones, ostinato and melodies. These could relate to
themes they are working on in the class; they could provide the musical accompaniment
for storytelling, poetry or dance.

Summary of key points

- Music education is a statutory National Curriculum subject.
- The National Curriculum focuses on musical behaviours: composing, performing, listening and appraising.
- Children should also learn *about* music: notation, musical language and theory (including standard notation), and music history.
- There are some key principles in teaching singing that can promote efficient teaching and musical progress.
- Music making can begin with very simple, rhythmic, starting points.
- Ofsted and the government recognise that music is a difficult subject for many schools to teach. For this reason, money has been invested in developing music hubs that can offer help both to individual teachers and to schools.
- Class teachers can do much to promote enthusiasm for music. Teachers do not have to be expert musicians to promote musical development in their children. They do need to have an open mind, to have a go and to try to talk with the children as fellow musicians.

- Children should have a broad musical experience that doesn't just focus on learning to play an instrument and singing.
- Good music lessons are dominated by music making. They have a good sense of flow and the learning objectives are clearly defined.
- Teachers should try to establish music as a central part of school life, with regular opportunities for performance.
- Music should be purposeful and fulfilling. It is often fun, but at other times it requires focused concentration.

References

Department for Education and Employment (DfEE) (1999) *The National Curriculum Handbook for Primary Teachers*. London: DfEE.

DfE (2013) *National Curriculum in England: Music Programmes of Study*. Online at: www.gov.uk/government/publications/national-curriculum-in-england-music-programmes-of-study (accessed August 2014).

Elliot, D.J. (ed.) (2005) *Praxial Music Education: Reflections and Dialogues*. Oxford: Oxford University Press.

Office for Standards in Education (Ofsted) (2012) *Music in Schools: Wider Still and Wider*. London: Ofsted.

Stunell, G. (2006) The policy context of music in English primary schools: how politics didn't help music. *Research Studies in Music Education*, 26, 1, pp. 2–21.

Swanwick, K. (1999) *Teaching Music Musically*. London: Routledge.

Welch, G.F. (1986) A developmental view of children's singing. *British Journal of Music Education*, 3, 3, pp. 295–303.

Wenger, E. (1998) *Communities of Practice: Learning, Meaning, and Identity*. Cambridge: Cambridge University Press.

Online sources

www.qca.org.uk (accessed August 2014)
www.singup.org (accessed August 2014)

9 Physical education

Mike Goulding

Physical education can develop lifelong passion for a particular physical activity such as running, dance, swimming or a sport. It can help children become healthier both in body and in mind, and with the Olympics in London 2012 the power of physical education was felt through the enthusiasm of the nation, who demanded a legacy that we could all be proud of. Primary physical education can contribute to that legacy and help develop physically confident and fit children that develop into physically confident and fit adults.

This chapter will look at the identity of physical education, the primary curriculum and the pedagogy of physical education, and finally will give ideas for activities for the teacher's toolkit. This approach aims to give everyone involved in teaching physical education the confidence to deliver high-quality lessons.

The identity of physical education

In 1999, physical education was described in the revised National Curriculum as follows:

> Physical education develops pupils' physical competence and confidence, and their ability to use these to perform in a range of activities. It promotes physical skilfulness, physical development and a knowledge of the body in action. Physical education provides opportunities for pupils to be creative, competitive and to face up to different challenges as individuals and in groups and teams. It promotes positive attitudes towards active and healthy lifestyles.
>
> (DfEE 1999: 15)

This was a welcome definition in an area where sometimes it is difficult to get a consensus as to what physical education is and what it does. It is quite possible that, when asking a room full of people what they think physical education is, that they could all give a different answer. This is fine but I would maintain, too, that we need to also agree on some common ground to make the argument for physical education stronger.

In more recent times physical literacy has been put forward as a worthwhile approach. Whitehead defines this approach as 'the motivation, confidence, physical competence, knowledge and understanding to value and take responsibility for engagement in physical activities for life' (2014). This approach sees physical education as more than just learning skills as it places the learner as an important part of the approach who must take responsibility for their engagement in physical activities.

Learning to move and moving to learn are closely aligned to physical literacy. The association for physical education (AfPE) states that:

> Learning to move is about the learning of the movement skills required for participation in different types of physical activities. Moving to learn is not only about the learning needed for participation in physical activities but also the learning integrated with other aspects of school learning within and beyond the curriculum.
>
> (Association for Physical Education 2014)

This makes a case for physical education being more than just learning about physical skills but also that it can promote learning through movements. It might be that children can learn about the benefits of exercise and look at the health issues connected with lack of exercise. Physical education may allow children to communicate with others while taking part in activities. This will improve their social skills as they become more confident communicators.

Reflection points

- *What do you think are the aims of physical education?*
- *What are the benefits of physical education to children?*
- *Begin to build your own philosophy of physical education?*

The physical education curriculum

Physical education has gone through many changes and had numerous initiatives thrust upon it in recent years. It was included in the National Curriculum in 1988, which made it statutory at all key stages. This continued in the revised curriculum of 1999 with a suggested activity time of a minimum of two hours a week.

The importance of physical education was also demonstrated in 2002 when money was made available to primary schools to improve physical education provision. The Physical Education and School Sport and Community Links Strategy (PESSCL) gave £1.5 billion to improve the participation of primary children. The target of a public service agreement was that, by 2008, 80 per cent of children would be participating in two hours of high-quality physical education per week (DfE 2003, cited in Ofsted 2005). This strategy became Physical Education and School Sports and Young People (PESSYP) in 2008, and aimed to give children five hours of physical education and school sport made up of three hours' extra-curricular activity and two hours' curriculum activity.

A more recent initiative has been the deployment of further funds for primary physical education given to all primary schools. This has been promised until 2020 but of course the government may change, hence so may the policy. This said, the money is guaranteed until 2016. The idea is that schools will use the funding to improve a primary school's physical education. It could be curriculum physical education, school sport or the fitness of children. This is a welcome initiative and gives schools the opportunity to demonstrate the impact they have made using the funding (Wilkinson and Colin, 2013).

In the 2014 National Curriculum (DfE 2013), physical education is statutory at all key stages. This demonstrates its importance as it is only one of two foundation subjects that must be taught at all four key stages. The National Curriculum for physical education (2013) has slimmed down programmes of study and the levels of attainment are to be removed. It is important to remember that the National Curriculum for physical education is a minimum requirement and the school provision can and should exceed it.

Subject content of the National Curriculum

The six areas of physical education consisting of games, gymnastics, dance, athletics, outdoor and adventurous activities (OAA), and swimming may not be as prominent in the 2014 National Curriculum for physical education (DfE 2013), but it would be advantageous to provide children with as wide a range of activities as possible.

The subject content for Key Stage 1 is based on the development of core movements. Agility, balance and coordination should be extended during this key stage. Children should be given opportunities to work on their own and with others (DfE 2013). Competition is given a more prominent role, with children taking part in attacking and defending.

In Key Stage 2 these basic movements are built upon and pupils should continue to implement and develop a broader range of skills, learning how to use them in different ways and to link them to make actions and sequences of movement. They should enjoy communicating, collaborating and competing with one another. They should develop an understanding of how to succeed in different activities and sports, and learn how to evaluate and recognise their own success (DFE 2013: 181).

When teaching a high-quality physical education lesson the teacher should always plan to provide opportunities for children to:

- acquire and develop skills
- select and apply skills, tactics and compositional ideas
- evaluate and improve performance
- develop knowledge and understanding of fitness and health.

Acquiring and developing skills, and selecting and applying them, can be incorporated into a typical four-part lesson:

- warm up
- development – acquiring and developing skills
- applying – selecting and applying skills, tactics and compositional ideas
- warm/cool-down.

Evaluating and improving performance should also be built in to every lesson but it should be a quick worthwhile activity that does not have the children inactive for too long. I tend to have children working in pairs where one child can observe another and then feed back to them. The children should feed back two things that the child did successfully and one thing they could improve. The children then swap roles and the process is repeated. The secret of this working is that the children know what quality is. This means that the teacher needs to make sure that the children know what a good forward roll looks like or what a good chest pass looks like. The children need to have the vocabulary and the knowledge to feed back to their partner in a meaningful way. This whole process should take five minutes maximum.

Knowledge of fitness and health can be built in to every lesson. It might be in the warm-up, where you can ask the children questions such as:

- Why do we do a warm-up?
- What do you feel like after the warm-up?
- What are the short-term effects of exercise?

Also the children could be asked questions throughout the lesson, such as:

- Why do you think exercise is good for you?
- Why do we need to warm down?

Health and safety

This is an important part of physical education. If the activities that you plan are well organised and any risks have been assessed then the lessons can be challenging and adventurous. The environment children are going to work in needs to be free from trip or slip hazards and appropriate for the activity. The teacher needs to have good subject knowledge and know how any apparatus should be used. The teacher should demonstrate to the children how the apparatus is used correctly and safely. All risks should be shared with the children so they are aware of them. You may put markers down or ropes to mark off an area of the playground that is unsuitable or where a trip hazard cannot be moved.

Another important aspect is to let children know your expectations. They need to know that, when they enter the hall, they must follow your directions. They need to know from the start what you expect. If you leave no grey areas and your instructions are clear then the children will be clear on what they need to do to remain safe.

The Association for Physical Education (AfPE) has been the place to go to for advice on health and safety issues in PE. A recommended text is *Safe Practice in Physical Education and School Sport* (AfPE 2012). This will give advice on all issues of safety, from suitable clothing right through to providing risk assessment forms that practitioners can use to decide the risks in an activity and how they can be removed or lessened.

Reflection points

- *Think about how you teach physical education: do you include health-related exercise; do you build in peer evaluation?*
- *What are the most important strategies to maximise children's learning?*
- *Think of the safety issues in two different lessons you have taught or observed.*

The pedagogy of physical education

In this part of the chapter I will be exploring different teaching approaches that can be used in physical education. I will look at ideas that improve the children's learning and understanding of physical education.

Teaching styles in physical education

Mosston and Ashworth (1994, cited in Lawrence 2012) believe there are a number of questions that need to be asked before deciding on a teaching style.

These are:

- What are my learning objectives? What do I want my pupils to achieve?
- What is the best method to use to achieve these objectives?
- How should I structure my teaching?
- How should I organise the learning?
- How do I motivate my children?
- How do I encourage social interactions and thinking?
- How will I know that I have achieved my objectives?

The teaching styles put forward by Mosston and Ashworth range from the command style, where all the decisions are made by the teacher, right along the spectrum to self-teach, where the child would be teaching themselves and making all the decisions. There are 11 styles in all and the styles form a spectrum of teaching approaches, with the main focus being the teacher's relationship with the children in terms of who makes the decisions in learning.

The 11 styles are:

- command – teacher makes decisions; often used when there is a lot of information to give out, or as a behaviour management tool

- practice – the children are set a task and then practise a skill such as throwing and catching
- reciprocal – children work together to increase their learning
- self-check – children identify their own strengths and weaknesses
- inclusion – children select their own task and evaluate the completed task
- guided discovery – children are given questions to help them progress to completing a task
- convergent – the children must solve problems through trial and error
- divergent – the children give different answers to a problem; they are making the decisions
- individual programme – the child develops an individual programme, e.g. warm-up routine
- learner initiated – this builds on the previous style, with the child evaluating their individual programme
- self-teach – here the child teaches her/himself.

These descriptions are obviously shortened from Mosston and Ashworth's original styles, but they still give us a flavour of the different teaching styles that can be used in physical education. It would be interesting for teachers to try out different styles to see the outcomes. It is easy as busy teachers to take all the decisions and stick to the command or practice style, and these are very useful styles, but if we are to give children greater independence in their learning then we need to use a range of styles that suit the activity the children are participating in. Also we need to be sure that the children are ready to take greater responsibility for their learning in physical education.

Creativity

One way of bringing creativity into a lesson is by allowing the children to make up their own game using selected equipment; this could be a cricket bat and a large sponge ball. These two pieces of equipment don't usually go together so the children will have to think how they can incorporate the two pieces of equipment in a game. In allowing the children to devise a game, we are giving them greater freedom to think and take control of their learning. The children decide on the size of the pitch or court that they play on. They devise the rules of the game. They should be discouraged from devising a game that is based on a well-known team game. In our example I would try to direct the children away from a straightforward cricket game with the only difference being a large sponge ball.

Differentiation

It must be an aim that all children are catered for in our lessons. One very simple way of differentiating activities is the STTEP method (Pickup and Price 2007). This approach allows the teacher to adapt a game to make it easier or harder for individuals or a group of children. This differentiation by task can be very simple yet very effective. It often has been a real revelation to some of my trainee teachers when they see how easy it can be to differentiate in PE.

For STTEP to work the equipment available must be appropriate and safe. There are many suppliers of equipment that provide colourful, light, quality resources. If we want

Table 9.1 STTEP table

S	Space	Make the space bigger or smaller, or a different shape. By making the space bigger in small-sided invasion games, it reduces the pressure on the attackers and gives more space to attack
T	Time	Some skills can be performed slowly or quickly, making the task more or less demanding. Faster-paced skills are not always more difficult – performing a gymnastic sequence as slowly as possible will create greater challenges for accuracy and control
T	Task	The specific requirements of each task can be altered. Children of differing abilities can be asked to perform specific tasks to help meet the same learning outcomes
E	Equipment	Equipment can be used to increase or lessen performance demands. A small, hard ball will be harder to hit in striking and fielding games than a larger, softer and slower-moving ball
P	People	Greater numbers of children involved in a task tend to make the group task more complex. A class dance becomes a more difficult choreographic exercise with all the children involved

children to produce quality outcomes then they must be provided with the tools to do it. The funds are available through the government's sport premium so the opportunity is there for schools to really provide quality and exciting resources for physical education, to make sure their children are motivated to make real progress in their learning.

The STTEP principle will also help with the important issue of inclusion in physical education. Vickerman maintains that teachers are 'required to work flexibly and creatively to design environments that are conducive to learning for all. This involves identifying potential barriers to learning teaching and assessment, whilst using strategies that offer access and entitlement to PE' (2010: 168).

To ensure that children are included in physical education lessons we need to make sure the area we are using is suitable for all children. If you think a space is too small or unsuitable then adapt the activity to suit the space you have, or change the space. This is always a consideration in terms of health and safety, e.g. we need enough space for children to move around safely and participate in a game, dance or gymnastic sequence. It is also important that children with learning needs in physical education are given the space and environment necessary so they can progress their learning as much as possible.

Reflection points

- *What teaching styles do you use in your PE lesson?*
- *Can you think of a style you would like to try?*
- *How would you use STTEP to make an activity easier or harder for children in your class?*
- *Can you think of children you have taught or are teaching that would benefit from a particular adaptation?*

The physical education teacher's toolkit

This part of the chapter will provide you with ideas and activities to use in PE lessons. They are ideas that have been developed, designed and adapted from a range of teaching and coaching experiences. You will benefit most from these ideas by trying them and reflecting on them, and finally adapting them so that they are activities that you feel have the greatest impact on children's learning in physical education.

A physical education lesson will usually consist of:

- a warm-up
- development of skills
- application of skills
- warm/cool-down.

This format is only one approach and there are other structures that can be followed, but I have used this as it is the easiest approach for teachers who are not trained specialists in physical education. Another approach is to play a game first and then develop skills later as they are identified or a particular skill breaks down. This four-part lesson can be used for all areas of physical education; this is reassuring for teachers and trainee teachers who have to plan and teach physical education lessons.

The first group of ideas are for use in the warm-up. The warm-up should take no longer than five minutes. This is where we want to get the children raising their heart rate and stretching their muscles. This allows children to develop good habits in readying their body for exercise. It is also the start of the lesson, so if we can engage and allow the children to buy in to the lesson then it is a great start. We can do this by making warm-ups fun and inclusive so every child feels part of the lesson and is wanting more of what we are offering. I have used all the ideas in the following section and found them to work with primary children. I hope you will take them and use them, but also reflect on them and improve or adapt them to suit your children.

Warm-ups

The bean game
One of my favourite warm-ups is the bean game. This is where you shout out a type of bean and the children perform an action. If the teacher says runner bean, then the children run. If the teacher says jumping bean, then the children jump. There are many different types of bean but here are a few that have proved popular:

- baked bean – tuck into a ball shape
- beans on toast – lie on the floor
- chilli bean – shiver like you are cold
- string bean – stretch as tall as you can
- French bean – say something in French
- jelly bean – shake like a jelly.

I am sure you and your class can think of even more creative beans. This is a warm-up that children love from reception to Year 6 and it allows you to give the children an enjoyable beginning of the lesson. It also involves stretching and travelling, which will raise the heart rate.

Traffic lights

This is an old favourite, which again you can adapt or add your own ideas. Green is obviously go, but you can get the children to travel in different ways, e.g. running, skipping, walking. Amber is jogging on the spot, but again you can choose an action for the children to do on the spot. Red is stop and again you can get the children to freeze or you can get them to perform a stretch. According to the age of the children you are teaching, you can add or take away commands. Here are some commands that can be used:

- blue flashing light – perform a star jump
- motorway – children run quickly in the same direction
- taxi – children link arms and run around with a partner
- tunnel – children crawl on hands and feet.

Gears

The objective of this game is to warm up the body, develop a marked change of pace in the children, and encourage the children to dodge and react to other children. The children begin in gear 1 (walking slowly), then move on to gear 2 (quick walking), 3 (jogging), 4 (running), 5 (sprinting). The teacher calls out gear 1, 2, 3, etc., in order. Once they have got the idea, the teacher can switch from gear 1 to 4, 3 to 5, etc.

Teaching points: look for quick changes of direction, moving into space to avoid others. Progression: use different actions for each gear – for example, side-stepping, jumping.

Cats and mice

The objective of this game is to practise dodging skills and improve balanced movement. The equipment needed is a set of bibs. The teacher divides the class in half: cats and mice. The mice tuck a bib into the back of their shorts (a tail) and start inside the playing area. Cats line up outside the area and are sent in two at a time to steal a tail. Once they have taken a tail, they tag the next cat that is sent into the playing area. Any mouse losing a tail must leave the playing area. Encourage players to make a definite dodge move to avoid others. Look for quick changes of direction, pushing off on the outside foot, and using hips and shoulders to keep balanced. This game can be progressed by all cats going into the playing area at the same time (increases the number of taggers). This will make the game much busier so be aware of health and safety in relation to your class and their abilities.

Domes and dishes

The objective of this popular game is to practise running, turning, bending down and choosing pathways. The only equipment needed is a set of markers. The teacher splits the class in half, one half are domes and the other half are dishes. The children take a marker and put it in the playing area as a dish or a dome. Then, on the teacher's command, the dishes all run around turning over the markers so they are dishes. The domes also run around and turn the markers over so that they are domes. The game continues until the teacher says stop. I would suggest no longer than a minute as it is a real pulse raiser. When the children have all stopped (and are not touching any markers) then the teacher or a chosen child can count the number of domes and number of dishes. The winner is the team with the most domes or dishes. The game can be repeated using a shorter time span. You can make the game harder for some children by making them turn over only certain coloured markers. This will present faster children with a challenge.

The second area for ideas is developing skills. The development of skills can take place in games, gymnastics, dance, athletics, swimming, and outdoor and adventurous activities. I will again provide some activities that have worked in school and have allowed children to enjoy PE while acquiring and developing skills. The activities are for invasion games in this instance. When teaching these lessons I am convinced that every child should have their own equipment, to maximise their opportunities to acquire and develop the skill being developed. The idea is for children to have the opportunity to develop their skills individually at first, e.g. dribbling a football or dribbling a hockey ball. Try to give the children some time to explore with their ball or apparatus. Then children can work in pairs to practise passing a ball. This can be done while they are still and then they can progress to passing and then moving. The ideas below are a mixture of individual, paired and team activities.

Developing skills

Goals/gates

This game needs lots of little goals (use two markers to make a goal) to be set out on a playing area. The game consists of the children dribbling through the goals and, each time they go through a goal, they get a point. The idea is to encourage the children to dribble, keeping control of the ball or object and to pass through as many gates as possible. The area needs to be big enough to allow children to safely dribble through several goals. The advantage of this game is that the children can dribble a football, basketball or hockey ball. The children can even start off by just running through the goals. This can also be used to differentiate the activity for children who may struggle with dribbling a ball. The children are given one minute to pass through as many goals as possible. Then they can feed back to the teacher or a partner how many points they scored. Then the children can repeat the activity to see if they can beat their previous score. This means the children are entering into competition against themselves.

Swap partners

The objective of this game is to develop passing and receiving a pass. Also it aims to develop looking for a pass and moving to receive a pass. The game consists of the class being put into pairs. In their pairs, the children face each other, about two steps apart, and one of them has a ball. The person with the ball passes to their partner and then goes looking for a new partner. The person who received the ball stays still and waits until a new partner comes to them. When they have a new partner they then pass the ball to them and then they go looking for a new partner. It is amazing how much excitement this game generates by children having to pass and then look for a new partner. Encourage the children to be accurate with their passes and not to throw until a partner is ready to receive. The game can be changed by using a different pass or different-sized ball. The amount of throws can be changed before the child moves. Please note that the number of throws always needs to be odd for the game to work.

Ball skills

Ball handling fun drills with partner
Passing round the world, figure of eight, under and over.

Ball handling
One ball between two players. Players stand arm's length away, facing each other. Player A lightly places hands on head. Player B drops the ball from different heights in front of A, who tries to catch the ball before it hits the ground. The players take it in turns to catch the ball.

One ball between two players. Players stand facing each other about two metres apart. One, the attacker 'A', has the ball. The defender, 'D', runs quickly on the spot using small steps. A passes or drops the ball in any direction within arm's reach of D. D catches and returns to A.

One ball, one cone between two players. Players stand arm's length away, facing each other. They place the ball on the cone that is between them. Teacher shouts out various body parts – e.g. heads, shoulders, knees, bottom – and players have to touch this part with two hands. When the teacher calls 'ball', both players attempt to snatch the ball off the cone. Remind children to keep their body straight and to bend their knees when low.

The following games, ten-point hoops and piggy in the middle, relate to the QCA/DCSF schemes of work for games activities. By observing children carrying out these tasks, the teacher gets a visual snapshot of what the child can do, and so can track and plan pupils' progress in games activities.

Ten-point hoops
The objective of this game is to score points by throwing beanbags into a choice of two targets. The equipment needed consists of: two children, five beanbags, two hoops, one rope.

- Working in pairs, the children set up an area for their game with either a line marking or a rope for the halfway line and two hoops positioned on one side of the line as targets.
- The pupils stand on either side of the line, one as an attacker and one as a defender. The attacker aims to throw a beanbag into one of the hoops, moving around the area and throwing when they think they have dodged their opponent.
- The defender tries to stop the beanbag landing in the hoop. The attacker scores two points for each beanbag that lands in a hoop. After five throws, the defender becomes the attacker and tries to beat their opponent's score.

Teaching points: the children should move into different positions before throwing. They should throw with a suitable underarm technique, and move to try and intercept the beanbags. They can change speed and direction to outwit their opponent. Players should watch others' movements carefully. Also encourage children to describe what they have done or seen others doing. This will allow them to demonstrate that they understand how to play the game more successfully.

Piggy in the middle
This is a practice that is used in coaching and teaching invasion games when trying to encourage children to keep possession of a ball. This practice could be used in football,

rugby, netball, basketball and hockey. The activity takes place in a marked-out area (usually a rectangle or square). It consists of four children (three attackers and one defender).

- The attackers have to pass the ball among themselves and prevent the defender from touching the ball. The advantage is given to the attackers to try to allow them to make successful passes.
- If the defender is still getting the ball too easily then you could add another attacker or make the area bigger. I would not allow the attacker to move with the ball and then would encourage the other attackers to move into a space so that they can receive the ball.
- This is a very simple and effective activity to promote good passing and movement off the ball. The beauty of this practice is you can have several games going, all using different balls or equipment.

Mini-games

All of the skills learned in these practices can then be selected to use in games. When the children do take part in a game, it should always be a mini-game. This allows children to gain more experience and be more involved in the game because there are fewer players. For example, the passing and moving skills learned in piggy in the middle could be applied to a four vs four game. The game could take place on a marked-out court or pitch. One side would aim to pass the ball and attack the other team's goal. In this example they have to bounce it into a hoop to score a point. The game is still promoting passing so the player with the ball is not allowed to move, and in this instance we are passing the ball by throwing or bouncing it.

The skills we have developed and then applied to a mini-game have all been for invasion games, but the same approach can be used for dance, gymnastics, athletics, swimming and OAA. For instance, in gymnastics, the children can develop travelling actions and different balances. Then the travelling actions and balances could be applied to a sequence on the floor and mats, and finally onto apparatus. Likewise, dance actions can be developed and then linked together in a dance motif. The advantage of this is a consistent approach to developing skills and then applying them.

The final ideas are for warm/cool-downs, which should be done at the end of every lesson. This allows the children to calm their bodies down but also calm their minds down. The activity should involve only gentle exercise or stretching.

Warm/cool-downs

Letter shapes
The children jog gently around the space. When the teacher calls a letter, the children have to make that letter shape individually or with a partner or partners. Again this is not a new idea but it works and children are very creative in making the letter shapes.

Mirror stretching
Children are in pairs; one of them performs a stretch and their partner mirrors that stretch. They then swap roles and repeat the activity with another stretch. I usually let the children perform two stretches each.

Sticking together

The children jog around the room changing direction. When the teacher shouts 'knee' then they all must join knees with a partner or partners. The children jog around again until the teacher shouts elbow and then they must join elbows. The activity is repeated using different body parts. This is great fun for the children but be aware of safety.

Warm-downs can also include more gentle versions of warm-ups. All that needs to be remembered is the aim is to calm down the body and the mind.

Summary of key points

- Physical education is statutory at Key Stage 1 and 2 and, if taught through a variety of activities, it can have a real impact on the development of a child. The new National Curriculum recognises the importance of fundamental skills to the physical development of children. It also gives competition a more important role in primary physical education.
- Physical literacy is an approach to PE that recognises the confidence and enjoyment that participating in physical education can bring to a child. The approach aims to use this confidence and enjoyment as the motivation for children to continue participating in physical education throughout their life. This can lead to children and adults becoming more active, which can lead to healthier lives.
- All children should be included in physical education, and children who have a special educational need should participate in activities that are adapted to give them a meaningful experience. The differentiation of activities should be part of every PE lesson and should allow all children to gain success.
- A lesson should be well structured and include a warm-up at the beginning and a warm/cool-down at the end. The main lesson can be split into developing skills, and then applying those skills to a game, dance or gymnastic sequence.
- Teachers can employ different styles that give the children varying amounts of responsibility for decision making. Also teachers should encourage children to be creative in their work rather than always copying the teacher.
- Health and safety is important, but once all risks have been identified and minimised then lessons can be challenging and adventurous.

References

Association for Physical Education (2012) *Safe Practice in Physical Education and School Sport*. Leeds: Coachwise.

Association for Physical Education (2014) Advocacy and influence. Online at: www.afpe. org.uk (accessed August 2014).

Department for Education (DfE) (2013) *The National Curriculum for England Framework Document*. London: DfE.

DfEE (1999) *The Revised National Curriculum*. London: DfEE.

Lawrence, J. (2012) *Teaching Primary Physical Education*. London: Sage.

Ofsted (2005) *The Physical Education and School Sport and Community Links Strategy.* London: Crown.

Pickup, I. and Price, L. (2007) *Teaching Physical Education in the Primary School: A Developmental Approach.* York: Continuum.

Vickerman, P. (2010) Planning for an inclusive approach to learning and teaching. In Capel, S. and Whitehead, M. (eds) *Learning to Teach Physical Education in the Secondary School*, 3rd edn. London: Routledge.

Whitehead, M. (2014) Physical literacy definition. Online at: www.physical-literacy.org.uk (accessed August 2014).

Wilkinson, S. and Colin, J. (2013) Effective use of physical education and school sport premium. *Physical Education Matters*, Summer.

10 Religious education

Maggie Webster

Primary teachers are required to teach religious education (RE) at least once a week, and often this task is devolved to the teaching assistant during planning, preparation and assessment time, or to the trainee teacher. This is a shame as it suggests teachers do not understand the potential of RE. Religious education allows children and adults to challenge some of the narrow-minded views they experience in the media and in society about the choices people make and how they live, hence it is a useful subject that encourages the revision of stereotypes and so should be embraced by all. Creative RE encourages a collegiate and questioning classroom, and can develop thinking skills that are invaluable to life-long learning.

Tõõo be able to teach it well, having a good understanding of its purpose and how to teach in a way that is acceptable to your own and the children's ethical or religious standpoint is essential, and so this chapter explores religious education through its four key skills and the pedagogy of planning. It also offers a selection of toolkit ideas that you can adapt and use in a primary classroom, inspiring children to find their own answers to the big questions of life.

The identity of religious education

Ofsted's 2013 review of religious education noted that teachers did not necessarily understand the purpose of RE, and hence the lessons they saw lacked criticality and substance. To ensure RE is more than personal social and health education (PSHE) there needs to be a clear understanding of its essence, i.e. its purpose.

It is generally accepted that education should be about enabling children to be resilient, resourceful learners who are able to adapt and use a varied skill set so that they can cope with a future we cannot plan for (Claxton 2008). Religious education is the same, but it includes an additional set of skills that enable children to grow into citizens who acknowledge various lifestyles, are respectful of choice and yet are not afraid to have open, respectful dialogue about difference.

To be able to achieve this, a teacher needs to be aware that religious education is not about telling children what to believe but allowing them to have an informed opinion on what they are curious about. The essence of the subject therefore is to encourage children to explore what it means to be human.

Identity in a community school

In a community school, Religious Education explores the six world faith traditions of Buddhism, Christianity, Hinduism, Islam, Judaism and Sikhism. By the end of a child's primary school career they should have explored each faith in some depth and be able to make connections between them. It is likely, however, that schools may explore other faith traditions, such as Jehovah Witness, because a child in the school may belong to that faith. It is essential therefore that staff are informed as to how Jehovah Witnesses practise their faith so to model respect and help remove prejudice.

The school ethos and religious education scheme of work should encourage children to reflect upon all faiths and non-faiths, and form their own opinion. Collective worship should be non-denominational, whereby children are asked to consider a poem or prayer but not take part in any form of religious practice.

Identity in a faith school

A faith school has a strong identity that is affiliated to a religion, be that Buddhist, Christian, Hindu, Islamic, Jewish or Sikh. Religious education within such schools is focused upon that particular religion rather than the six major faith traditions, and the identity therefore is to advocate one particular belief system above others.

With the growth of Free Schools it is interesting to see more charities and denominations acquiring schools that have a religious focus and parents choose such schools for this reason, feeling that the religion underpins everything else. A faith school's identity is closely linked to the ethos, and the aim of the faith schools' religious education syllabus is to support children into becoming members of that particular faith community. Hence children learn about the theology of that faith and what it means to be a person who believes in its values.

A faith school in the UK will also explore other religions, however teaching about a religion that is different to the school's identified faith is not a requirement and so many schools look at another faith either because the school is situated in a multicultural area or to encourage religious tolerance. Since 9/11 and 7/7 most faith schools in the UK tend to explore Islam.

Religion in the twenty-first century

Abrams, Yaple and Weiner (2010) state that census data suggest organised religion is on the decline, possibly implying that, soon, people's affiliation and interest in religion will wane and then disappear. This raises the question of whether there is any value to studying religion if no one is religious. However, others suggest that there seem to be more links between theology, religion, spirituality and popular culture than ever (Detweiler 2010; Wagner 2012). Examples of this are in TV programmes such as *Homeland* and *Supernatural*; within music lyrics and videos such as Lady Gaga's *Judas* and Robbie Williams' *Jesus in a Campervan*; and within books such as the Twilight and Harry Potter series, and the Manga Messiah books. All of this suggests that interest in religion isn't waning but growing. Indeed, since 2010, there have been many BBC programmes on primetime TV that have had a spiritual or religious focus.

Religion on the internet and within popular culture is an emerging phenomenon and there is a developing body of knowledge that has tried to explain the reasons behind its popularity (see, for example, Brashar 2001; Dawson and Cowan 2004; Mazur and McCarthy 2011). This could mean that people's interest in religious and spiritual enquiry is still there but the nature of exploring and investigating it is different. Many people would suggest they are spiritual rather than religious, and may only be religious in a cultural way, i.e. attending a wedding or a christening. This has an influence on what religious education is. The identity of religious education in the twenty-first century is likely to be very different to that of the twentieth century because of the digital global world we live in. As teachers we should acknowledge the changing religious world and realise that dismissing religion purely because it seems to be on the decline in census data is limited thinking.

The identity of religious education is to encourage children's search for what it means to be human, and so we should be mindful of how religion is affected by popular culture – to simply see RE as the production of facts about traditional religion is a little narrow minded. Religious education can be a fabulous subject if children are allowed to enquire for themselves into why people choose to live and act in the way they do.

Reflection points

- *Consider how you would adapt the curriculum and your medium-term plan (MTP) so that RE reflects society and what is of interest to children.*
- *Reflect on your own opinions of faith and whether these affect your teaching of RE. What will you do to ensure you encourage children to decide on their own opinion and not be overly influenced by others?*

The religious education curriculum

The content of the religious education curriculum within community schools can be found in the Local Authority Syllabus that has been created by the Standing Advisory Council for Religious Education (SACRE) and is updated every five years. Every local authority has to have an RE syllabus and each syllabus is different because the content reflects the religious demographic within that community.

This has caused confusion for many trainee teachers because they cannot find the 'Programmes of Study' or 'Attainment Targets' within the National Curriculum and so conclude that it does not have to be taught. Unless their placement school directs them towards the Local Authority Syllabus, they are at a loss as to what to teach and how to teach it. Yet religious education is a statutory subject and what is taught is dependent on where you live in the country. The debate about whether religious education, or religion in general, should be a statutory subject has been discussed for a while (see, for example, White 2004; Crush 2007) and it is still considered when there is a curriculum review (Staffroom 2014), but currently religious education remains within the wedding party but, as yet, is still not on the top table.

Faith schools have their own syllabus that is not community based but faith based. So, for example, Roman Catholic schools will use the syllabus 'Come and See', 'Here I Am' or 'The Way the Truth and the Life', and value religious education as a core subject not a foundation subject; it is therefore given more curriculum time.

What all syllabi (faith or community) seem to include, however, are the two Attainment Targets:

- Attainment Target 1 – Learning *About* Religion
- Attainment Target 2 – Learning *From* Religion.

Attainment Target 1 (AT1) requires children to learn facts and develop subject knowledge about names, places, practices etc., while Attainment Target 2 (AT2) encourages them to reflect on what those practices and facts mean to them personally.

In 2004 the Quality and Curriculum Authority (QCA) produced the Non-Statutory Framework for Religious Education, which explained this in detail, and SACREs and faith communities used this as a guide and reference to help them create their own syllabi. Since then, further guidelines (DSCF 2010) have been produced to direct teachers towards considering the purpose of RE, yet it seems that religious education is still poorly taught and teachers' confidence in how to teach it creatively is still lacking (Religious Education Council for England and Wales 2013).

The pedagogy of religious education

Four key skills in RE

This section explores how to plan religious education through the four key skills of communication, enquiry, reflection and thinking, so that lessons encourage children to become religiously considerate, informative and critical, and dispelling the general criticism of RE that teachers do not provide children with the opportunity to engage with the facts and reflect on what they mean to society and how they may relate to themselves (Baumfield 2012).

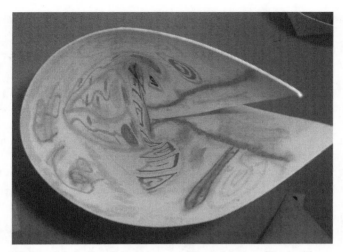

Figure 10.1 A child's interpretation of being filled with the Holy Spirit

Communication

This is the first of the four key skills. Children can communicate what they know and understand about a concept in written form, non-written form or verbally. For example, a child can communicate what they know through writing, discussion, question and answer, dance, drama, art or music. Often children are asked to complete worksheets or write what they know and understand, yet this can occasionally become a barrier for the child. When the child is encouraged to communicate what they know in a variety of ways, then they usually present a more honest and reflective answer.

Figure 10.1 offers a good example of creative communication. The scheme of work required Child A to imagine she was a disciple and write how she felt about being filled with the Holy Spirit. She found the writing difficult and wrote a sentence in 30 minutes. She was then asked to draw and verbally explain how a disciple might feel when filled with the Holy Spirit. She was able to describe her feelings through the colours she chose and she told the teacher that the disciple would feel 'colourful and excited'. She then said that she had turned her paper into a cone because 'the inside is changed but the outside looks the same'.

Enquiry

This is the second key skill and encourages children to ask 'big questions' that do not have a set answer. This can be challenging at times as some children (and teachers) like to have a fixed answer, but the beauty of religious education is that there are many answers and it is up to the individual to decide which they feel is the correct one for them. Usually a good way to encourage big questions is to use 'I wonder ...', as this raises the question without it suggesting that an answer is expected.

Reflection

This is an internal personal process and can be difficult to provide time for within a noisy busy school, but reflection requires quiet to consider a particular 'I wonder ...' question or topic. It is a skill that can be developed with practice but also a method, so the teacher needs to ensure there is time for reflection either inside or outside the classroom. Reflection requires the child and adult to be silent for a period of time so that they can think about a given topic, question or focus.

Thinking

This is an external process and links to communication. It requires the child to communicate in some form what they know and understand. Thinking skills can be taught, but in religious education this is mainly related to deciding how the children can communicate what they know and understand to you, themselves or one another. It can be related to the reflection task, but not always.

In the current assessment culture, many teachers are concerned about recording what the children have learned, but there are many ways of doing this. Think creatively and it is possible to record the various ways of communicating a child's understanding of religious education so that it is not necessary to rely on written output – for example, take photographs, video or recordings of what the children say, photographs of their artwork, freeze-frames, discussion groups, make Post-it notes of verbal responses, etc. Think creatively about assessment and then the lessons are likely to be creative too (Webster 2010).

Planning for religious education

One of the best planning models for religious education is from Lancashire's RE syllabus. Teachers are encouraged to plan through the 'Field of Enquiry Model', which is useful for medium- and short-term planning, and provides a balance of AT1 and AT2 (see Crabtree, Harrison and Webster 2010 for more information). All quadrants should be used within an MTP so that both attainment targets are catered for.

Medium-term planning

The model is a grid with four squares and each quadrant represents a lesson (see Table 10.1). The first lesson is likely to be related to the SHE quadrant. This lesson would explore AT2 and be implicitly religious in nature. For example, the lesson may be about how people celebrate. The children list and sort photographs of birthdays, anniversaries, cake, drink, presents, and so on, to look at the characteristics of celebration.

Table 10.1   Field of enquiry 1

SHE Shared Human Experience AT2	LTR Living Religious Traditions AT1
THEME – focused question	
SPM Search for Personal Meaning AT2	B&V Beliefs and Values AT1

The next three lessons are then related to the LRT and B&V quadrants. They are explicitly religious, and explore what people of faith do and why. For example:

- What do Christians do to celebrate Christmas?
- What do Hindus do to celebrate Diwali?
- What do Jews do to celebrate Hanukkah?

The final lesson in the medium-term plan would be the SPM quadrant, and would include reflections and activities about what the child thinks celebration means to them personally. This could be explicitly or implicitly religious.

Short-term planning

This model can also be used for a short-term lesson plan and it isn't necessary to use all of the quadrants in every lesson. The lesson could be focused on AT1 or AT2 or both, and leads in to the next lesson. Table 10.2 shows an example of a short-term plan.

Table 10.2 Field of enquiry 2 – short-term plan

SHE **Shared Human Experience**	LTR **Living Religious Traditions**
	Intro – what do we know about the Christmas story? List the events in order
	AT1
THEME – focused question	
SPM **Search for Personal Meaning**	B&V **Beliefs and Values**
Main activity – freeze-frame in groups; give each one part of the Christmas story – personal and group interpretations (can be modern) Show them in order of events to the rest of the class	**Conclusion** – why do Christians see this as an important event? Lead in to next lesson to explore the Christian Christmas message and why it is significant
AT2	AT1

Creativity in religious education

AT2 actively encourages children to make connections between religious practices, opinions and beliefs. It can enthuse children's passions about specific concepts that resonate with them individually, and I would argue that creativity is grounded within religious education and a key pedagogical approach.

There are many definitions of what creativity is and it seems to be a popular concept linked to the creative arts. However, creativity isn't solely about painting or being musical; it is about a child learning creatively through their environment and being creative through communicating their understanding in any way they wish (Webster 2010: 2).

Ken Robinson would suggest that creativity is finding one's 'element' (2009: 21) and that, when someone has a passion for something, they become more creative and successful at it. Moreover, he notes that, within the current education system, children seem to be 'educated out of' creativity so they forget how to make connections and hence lose their passion. It is essential therefore that RE teachers use creative teaching methods that enable children to explore their ideas, questions and passions in order for them to remain creative thinkers.

Reflection points

- *Make a list of the themes that you could use for RE and that may be useful to develop the four key skills of RE. Use the Non-Statutory Framework for RE or/and your local authority syllabus as a guide.*
- *Write a medium-term plan using the Field of Enquiry Model.*

The religious education teacher's toolkit

The RE toolkit is mainly a set of ideas that you can use in the classroom, yet they can seem like gimmicks if you do not reflect on how to plan for them, consider the skills that are being developed, and the purpose and value of religious education as a subject. Each of the ideas below can be used in a faith or community school and adapted for various key stages.

Communication

To encourage communication through discussion you may wish to group children into expert groups (sometimes known as rainbow groups) and also use the technique of 'snowballing' where children start a discussion in pairs then continue it within a four then in an eight, then sixteen, etc. You can also encourage verbal communication through talk partners, talk buttons, talk tokens, etc. (see Webster 2011 for more ideas on grouping children so as to develop communication skills).

For written communication you can use mind-mapping to explore ideas, Post-it notes for questions, or stimuli such as scenarios asking children to imagine they are a Christmas angel who has to write on their job sheet at the end of the day.

Non-written communication involves children communicating their ideas through music, drama, dance, sculpture or abstract painting. Each of the four key skills of RE relates in some way to communication. The following activities should help you see various ways of communicating what a child knows, understands and can do in RE.

Enquiry

What does it tell me? (AT1)
- Know: What the picture is about?
- Understand: That there is information in a painting about religion
- Do: Create a research question

Place the children in mixed-ability groups of three and give the pen to the child who has the lowest capabilities in English. This child also needs to be in the centre of the group of three.

Provide each group with a religious painting or icon – Margaret Cooling (2000) has lots of good examples – and ask them to list the answers to the following questions.

1. *What does it tell me?* Be literal, i.e. there is a red dragon, there is a man, woman, etc.
2. *What doesn't it tell me?* Be literal, i.e. it doesn't tell me who the man or woman is or why there is a dragon.
3. *What do I want to find out?* The children list as many things as they want to find out, then they choose one focus and start to research that question to see if they can find the answer.

This activity encourages questioning skills and you will be amazed at some of the deep and unusual questions that they create about the painting. It is also a scaffold to research for we all know that searching for information on a large topic is difficult, but researching for something specific is interesting and much easier to do.

Philosophy for Children (AT1, AT2)

- Know: That advertising is used to 'sell' religion
- Understand: That people can be influenced by images
- Do: Debate popular culture and religion

Show some images that have been on advertising billboards around the world (e.g. those reproduced here in Figures 10.2 and 10.3).

The children vote as to whether they wish to discuss all three images or simply one of them. Using the Philosophy for Children (P4C) model (http://sapere.org.uk/), ask the children to create a question they wish to discuss.

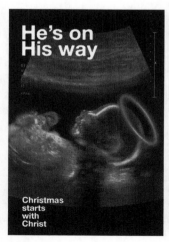
God baby 1

God baby 2

Figure 10.2 God baby
Note: These can be found via Google, but originated at www.churchads.net and www. christmasstartswithchrist.com (permission has been agreed with the owner, churchads.net)

Figure 10.3 Jesus image
Note: This image can be found via Google, but originated at www.churchads.net (permission agreed)

Order of P4C

1. The children sit in a circle.
2. Write a question related to the image on a Post-it then place it on the floor next to the image.
3. The questions are read aloud then placed into themes and broad areas of similarity.
4. The children then vote on which question they feel is the one they wish to discuss in more depth. The teacher is simply the facilitator and does not put in their opinion or direct the discussion.
5. After a process of elimination, one question is left as the one with the most votes and the child/children who wrote that question start(s) the discussion by explaining why they chose that question. The rest of the class begin to add their view and a focused debate happens. The teacher facilitates the discussion, looking for body language and other non-verbal signals to see who wishes to speak and who is reticent.

Hot-seating (AT1)

- Know: A particular religious story or character
- Understand: Parts of a religious event or story
- Do: Create 'big questions'

The children are placed in pairs and each pair is given a card with a question on it. They take it in turns to ask that question to the religious character who is sitting in the hot seat at the front of the class, i.e. Pontius Pilate, Judas, Sita, Rama. Once all the card-based questions have been asked, any child can ask a question and the teacher facilitates the discussion. If no one can think of a question, create a thought shower of questions and then ask the children to choose one to ask.

It is useful to note that, if you do hot seating without initially providing a set of cards, you are likely to have simple questions such as 'What is your favourite colour?' or 'What did you have for dinner?' The cards act as a scaffold so that the children are guided towards the sort of open-ended questions that are required for high-order thinking.

Before choosing which religious person is going to be in the hot seat it is worth knowing how your parents and children are likely to react. For example, some Christians would not mind you hot seating Jesus or God but others might; likewise some may be offended by hot seating the devil even though that would be an interesting interview!

A word of caution: do not put Allah or Mohammed into the hot seat as this would cause great offence to any Muslim.

Reflection

Handprints (AT2)

- Know: That I have a choice
- Understand: What I do affects others
- Do: To reflect on my legacy and the legacy of religious leaders

Share the *Pig of Happiness* by Edward Monkton and note how he made a decision to change things and make others happy.

Ask the children to sit quietly and, to avoid eye contact, close their eyes or focus on something in the room.

- They hold their thumb and reflect on – who makes you happy?
- They hold their index finger – how do they make you happy?
- They hold their middle finger – what have you done to make them happy?
- Then ring finger – how do you think people describe you?
- Finally, little finger – how do you describe yourself?

Ask them next to put their palms together (do not make it look like prayer):

- What sort of things do you want people to say about you?
- What can you do about it now?

The children draw their handprints on acetate, cut them out, then draw or write their responses in each finger. For the conclusion, discuss what they drew on their palm and what they want their legacy to be. Then stick the handprints on the window to make a display. The next lesson will develop so that you look at the characteristics of religious leaders and their legacy, e.g. Jesus, Buddha, Mohammed, Guru Nanak, Dalai Lama, the Pope.

Growing hope (AT2)
- Know: That positive thoughts can make you feel better
- Understand: That bad events can end
- Do: Reflect on negative events and make plans for a positive future

Ask the children to walk on their own around the playground or woods and, while walking, to reflect on things that have not always gone well for them and what they would like to change. While walking they do not talk with anyone.

On return the children are given a piece of red paper and they are asked to draw or write all the negative things they were thinking of when they were doing their reflective walk. They are then given a piece of green paper and a daffodil bulb or a summer bulb (depending on the time of year). They now write or draw all the things they want to happen in the future, i.e. their hope.

Once they have done both tasks, ask them to rip the red paper into tiny pieces and fold the green. Then take everyone outside to a flowerbed. The children mix the red paper into the earth, then take it in turns to read aloud their hope and plant the green paper underneath their bulb in the flowerbed. If you do not have a flowerbed you can use flowerpots and compost.

Over the months they will see the bulbs grow and the children will be reminded that out of negativity and fear, hope and love will grow. The set of lessons after this lesson could look at how Jesus felt in the Garden of Gethsemane and in the wilderness, and explore how he turned his negative thoughts into positive ones. Also you could explore Pagan ritual related to the power of 3 (i.e. what you send out comes back threefold), and/or Buddhism and Karma.

What would you give? (AT1, AT2)
- Know: That people of belief give up time, money or objects for their faith
- Understand: How difficult it is to sacrifice something
- Do: Consider what you would give up for someone

Watch the last scene of *Toy Story* where Andy gives away his toys to Bonnie. Ask the children to consider why he gave away his toys and how he felt about giving away his favourite toy, Woody.

Then ask them to be silent and reflect on what they have that is special, and then reflect on how they would feel if they had to give it away. Finally, ask them to consider who they love so much that they would give it to them, e.g. a family member, teacher, friend, God. After the reflection, explain to the children that Easter is about how the Christian God gave His most precious item (His son) to Christians to show that he loves them very much.

They then create their special object out of plasticine and reflect on who they would give it to. If you are doing this in a faith school you could ask the children to create something they would give God. Once they have created their object ask them to write on a Post-it note (or tell you and you write it) who they would give it to and why. The object can be an abstract concept or a physical object such as time, an open mind, confidence, etc.

The next lessons can explore various religions and how they all offer sacrifice in some way, e.g. Zakat or Ramadan in Islam; time in Sikhism; Lent in Christianity.

Thinking

Table of relevance (AT2)

- Know: That there is no correct answer
- Understand: That there is more than one answer to a question depending on one's perspective
- Do: Justify opinion and consider alternative views

Organise the children into mixed-ability groups of three. They are given a set of laminated cards that contain 10 to 15 statements and a piece of sugar paper. They have to read each card and decide if the statement is relevant to the question or not. If it is, they put it on the sugar paper and, if not, they put it on the outside of it.

They then read the cards on the paper again and 'diamond rank' them as to the most relevant and likely answer at the top to the least relevant and likely at the bottom. They then verbally justify why they chose this order.

Suggested question: Why did Jesus die?

Suggested statement cards:

1. Jesus was a political activist
2. Jesus was old
3. Pontius Pilate was afraid of the crowd
4. The story is in the Bible and so it is true
5. This is a made-up story
6. Jesus was unpopular
7. God was angry with Jesus
8. If Jesus didn't die Christianity wouldn't happen
9. Crucifixion was a popular punishment
10. Crucifixion was entertainment for people
11. Pontius Pilate wanted to stay popular
12. Jesus died to save Christians
13. His friends abandoned him
14. Religious leaders felt threatened by a new way of thinking
15. Jesus was saying he was a king

Loop game (AT1)

- Know: General facts about a religion
- Understand: That there are many similarities/differences within religion
- Do: Practise my subject knowledge, and develop thinking and listening skills

A loop game is very good at the start of a topic to assess pupils' prior knowledge and introduce them to key vocabulary and facts. It can also be used at the end of a topic to evaluate children's learning.

Divide the cards between the class (one between two so that they can support each other). The loop begins with reading aloud the 'Start' card, and the teacher encourages anyone who knows the answer to say it publicly. Whoever has the card with the answer reads aloud the 'I am ...' answer displayed on the card and then the question that is underneath. This continues around the room until the loop returns to the start.

Table 10.3   RE loop game

START Where do we get the objectives for RE from? **END** **I am a wise man**	**I am the Local Authority Syllabus and guidance from the Diocese** Who is the head of the Roman Catholic Church?	**I am the Pope** Who is the head of the Church of England?	**I am the Queen** What are the six major faith traditions that we teach in school?
I am Hinduism, Sikhism, Judaism, Islam, Christianity, Buddhism Who worships a god called Ganesh?	**I am a Hindu** What is the name of the Hindu festival of lights?	**I am a Diwali** What is the Jewish sacred text called?	**I am The Torah** Who prays five times a day?
I am a Muslim Who was betrothed to Joseph?	**I am Mary** What is the name of the Christian spring festival that remembers Jesus's death?	**I am Easter** What is the name of the Christian sacred space?	**I am a church** What is the Jewish festival that happens on a Friday called?
I am the Sabbath What is the Christian Great Commandment?	**I am Love your neighbour as you love yourself** Who told Mary in the Christian story that she was pregnant with Jesus Christ?	**I am the angel Gabriel** Who carried Mary to Bethlehem?	**I am the donkey** Who gave Jesus a gift of gold?

Do this twice and measure how long it takes. Try to see if they can recall the facts that are on the card without it being shared as a class and also how fast they can 'loop' the facts.

A short example of a generic loop game is shown in Table 10.3.

Eightfold Path (AT1, AT2)
- Know: About the Buddhist Eightfold Path
- Understand: That many religions have rules that they follow
- Do: Create own eight steps to happiness

Explain how various religions have rules that they live by, such as the 'Five Pillars of Islam', the 'Shema' in Judaism, the 'Great Commandment' of Christianity and the 'Five Ks' in Sikhism.

Explain to the children that Buddhists follow the 'Eightfold Path', which is related to the 'Four Noble Truths'. The Eightfold Path is eight steps that help a Buddhist reach enlightenment or, put very simply, happiness. The eight steps are:

1. Right Knowledge
2. Right Thought
3. Right Speech

4. Right Actions
5. Right Livelihood
6. Right Effort
7. Right Mindfulness
8. Right Concentration.

Place the children in mixed-ability groups of four or five, and give a step to each group. Ask them to define what they think the rule means, i.e. what is 'Right Concentration'?

Next ask them to work in a team to consider what they think are the steps to happiness. They have to produce a visual metaphor or 'still image' that represents their steps. Ideally they should have no more than eight steps to their happiness.

Finally, they communicate their steps to the rest of the class and the class have to work out what the group thinks happiness is. End the lesson with the video of the *Pig of Happiness* or *Love Monkey* by Edward Monkton.

Reflection point

- *Can you create any activities that might link to any other faith tradition such as Jehovah Witness or Paganism?*

Summary of key points

- Religious education is a statutory subject but not in the National Curriculum.
- SACRE creates the religious education syllabus for each local authority.
- Schools use the local authority syllabus to help them plan religious education.
- A faith school, such as a Roman Catholic school, follows its own syllabus.
- There are two Attainment Targets for religious education: Learning About Religion (AT1) and Learning From Religion (AT2).
- A faith school has a different religious identity to a community school.
- A faith school will focus upon its own belief systems before exploring any other religion in detail.
- Collective worship in a faith school encourages children to take part in religious practices.
- Collective worship in a community school encourages children to reflect on prayer but not to take part in religious practices.
- There are six major faith traditions (Buddhism, Christianity, Hinduism, Islam, Judaism, Sikhism) but schools may look at other religions from time to time.
- Popular culture, such as music, books and advertising, influence perceptions of religious education.
- The four key skills in religious education are communication, enquiry, reflection and thinking.
- The Field of Enquiry model is a good way to compose a medium- and short-term plan.
- Creativity is an effective pedagogy for religious education.

- Religious education in faith or community schools should be about children finding their own answers to the big questions in life.
- There are many toolkit ideas to teach religious education, fundamentally teachers need to encourage children to communicate what they know, understand and can do in ways that include written, verbal and non-written methods.

References

Abrams, D.M., Yaple, H.A. and Wiener, R.J. (2010) A mathematical model of social group competition with application to the growth of religious non-affiliation. *arXiv preprint arXiv:1012.1375*.

Baumfield, V. (2012) Understanding the wider context: meaning and purpose in religious education. *British Journal of Religious Education*, 34, 1, pp. 1–4.

Brashar, B. (2001) *Give Me that Online Religion*. San Francisco, CA: Jossey-Bass, Inc.

Cooling, M. (2000) *The Bible through Art. A Resource for Reaching Religious Education and Art*. London: Religious and Moral Press.

Claxton, G. (2008) *What's the Point of School? Discovering the Heart of Education*. London: Oneworld Publications.

Crabtree, J., Harrison, H. and Webster, M. (2010) From page to practice: creative RE using a locally agreed syllabus. *RE Source: A Journal of the National Association of Teachers of Religious Education*, Summer.

Crush, D. (2007) Should religious studies be part of the compulsory state school curriculum? *British Journal of Religious Education*, 29, 3, pp. 217–227.

Dawson, L. and Cowan, D. (2004) *Religion Online: Finding Faith on the Internet*. New York and London: Routledge.

Detweiler, C. (ed.) (2010) *Halos and Avatars: Playing Video Games with God*. Louisville, KY: Westminster John Knox Press.

DCSF (2010) *Religious Education in English Schools Non Statutory Guidance*. London: DCSF.

Mazur, E. and McCarthy, K. (2011) *God in the Details: American Religion in Popular Culture*. London: Routledge.

Ofsted (2013) *Religious Education: Realising the Potential*. London: Ofsted.

QCA (2004) *The Non-statutory Framework for Religious Education*. London: QCA.

Religious Education Council for England and Wales (2013) *A Review of Religions in England*. London: REC.

Robinson, K. (2009) *The Element: How Finding your Passion Changes Everything*. London: Penguin Books.

Staffroom (2014) The RE Subject Review for England: making a difference. *RE Today*, Spring, 14, pp. 40–41.

Wagner, R. (2012) *Godwired Religion, Ritual and Virtual Reality*. New York and London: Routledge.

Webster, M. (2010) *Creative Approaches to Teaching Primary RE*. Exeter: Pearson Ltd.

Webster, M. (2011) *Creative Activities and Ideas for Teaching Children with English as an Additional Language*. Exeter: Pearson Ltd.

White, J. (2004) Should religious education be a compulsory school subject? *British Journal of Religious Education*, 26, 2, pp. 151–164.

11 Learning outside the classroom

Cait Talbot-Landers

Learning Outside the Classroom (LOtC) is not a new or modern phenomenon, as those who were teaching in the 1970s and 1980s will recall. My own journey with LOtC started in the 1980s as a museum education officer highly influenced by the work of Lawrence Stenhouse and the Schools Council History Project. LOtC has its roots within the educational histories, such as active and experiential learning and is seen in curriculum principles from all around the world (Beames, Higgins and Nichol 2012).

However, since 2000 there has been a systematic raising of its profile through research, national and local initiatives, and the increasing acceptance on the part of the UK government that it can significantly contribute to the national educational agenda of raising attainment (including bridging the gap between groups of learners), and supporting the personal, social, cultural, moral, spiritual and physical development of children (DfES 2003, 2006; Research Centre for Museums and Galleries 2004; Children, Schools and Families Committee 2010; DfE 2013).

Learning Outside the Classroom (LOtC) and Learning Outdoors are educational terms that can be defined as 'The use of places other than the classroom for teaching and learning' (DfE 2006: 1). LOtC can be categorised into four zones:

1. the school grounds
2. the locality
3. day excursions
4. residential/expeditions.

Additionally a teacher needs to be mindful that LOtC incorporates informal learning settings (ILSs) – sometimes also referred to as informal education settings (IESs) – offering organised educational opportunities. Informal learning settings are organised sites offering specific educational and recreational opportunities for schools, families and the community. These include sites without designated onsite learning staff, but provide access and possibly onsite interpretation materials or offer online resources to support visits. Such sites include castles, small museums, historical and geographical landmarks, and places of worship.

Other ILSs provide a learning department offering programmes, workshops, events and resources to support school visits; organised educational provision within the ILS is a continuum. Alongside these are a range of landscapes and places that provide no organised educational interpretation or programmes, but offer teachers a rich learning environment and resources.

This chapter will focus upon supporting you through the use of the three-lens approach, to develop your knowledge and understanding of LOtC settings and spaces, and help you discover how to begin to effectively plan and embed LOtC experiences into your classroom practice.

The identity of Learning Outside the Classroom

On first reflection, the identity of LOtC can appear baffling and less clear than that of the individual foundation subjects. This is due to the multitude of identities contained within LOtC, which can make it appear complex.

Table 11.1 The setting: art gallery

Who uses it?	How and why do they use the gallery?
Art historian	To research different artists/movements and find out information about particular works. They are interested in different interpretations given to art, reflecting upon the history of art and how/why art has changed over time An art historian is engaged in research, writing books, TV programmes, delivering lectures/talks or working towards a qualification
The art appreciator	Enjoying and appreciating artworks, learning about different artists, genres and movements. They may attend tours and/or lectures, or visit the gallery on their own
The artist	Artists develop their own knowledge, skills and inspiration in art through learning from other artists
The creative practitioner	Creative practitioners such as writers, dancers, musicians and designers will use the gallery collection as inspiration for ideas that will be interpreted through their own discipline
The recreationalist	Recreationists may visit the gallery to eat, have a coffee, shop or participate in a specific workshop or event
The worker	The gallery requires many different roles in order to fulfil its purpose. The curator, learning team, front of house staff, etc. Curators are responsible for looking after the collection, researching it and making it accessible to the audience. They make the decision about what and how objects are exhibited, and write the interpretation materials.

The simplest way of viewing the identity of an informal learning space is to ask the questions 'Who uses this space?' and 'How and why do they use it?' This can then help you to begin to unpick what upon first inspection might appear bewildering. Table 11.1 presents the example of an art gallery. By identifying the different users of the gallery, a teacher can begin to see the different identities a gallery can have. This will help you to support your children as you begin to help them to understand and experience these identities themselves.

Bourdieu's conceptual framework to support understanding of identity within informal learning settings

In developing your understanding of identity within the different settings of LOtC, the theories and concepts drawn from the work of Piere Bourdieu (1991) can offer a framework with which to begin to analyse the individual identity. The key concepts are identified below.

Fields

Bourdieu contends that society can be viewed in terms of a series of social organisations and structures, which he defines as 'fields'. Schools, museums, galleries, etc., can all be identified as fields. Each field has its own agents, rhetoric (specific vocabulary), history, rules and specific games that are played within.

Agents

Each field has 'agents' or, to use a sporting analogy, 'players'. These are the groups that work or engage within the setting. They are the users of the settings referred to at the beginning of this chapter. The agents share, to varying degrees, an understanding and knowledge of the field in terms of recognising the different players within the field, understand the vocabulary specific to the setting, and recognise the games played and rules used.

The game

The 'game' is a concept that Bourdieu uses to identify and analyse what is happening within a field. It recognises that the agents are involved in playing different games using different rules for different purposes. The most effective way of understanding this concept is to reflect upon a field that you are part of, i.e. the primary school. Now consider the routine events/activities that take place within the school, e.g. lesson time, professional observations, Ofsted. Consider who is involved in these events: how does their behaviour alter, what is the purpose of the event, how and by whom is it judged to be successful? What are the success criteria by which the agent is judged to have 'won' the 'game'? These routine events, when analysed and defined using the concept of the game, can help us to have a clearer understanding of what is happening and why people act in the ways they do. It can support our greater understanding of the setting.

As teachers we are familiar with the 'field' of the school, its agents and its games but, when engaging with LOtC and using ILSs, we become just like sports teams who have to play away from home. We are always entering the 'field' of others to play a 'game' (the school visit) that is usually not familiar to us. This can appear daunting, and it is unsurprising that research (Stone 1992; Mathewson-Mitchell 2007) suggests that teachers can struggle and feel insecure when engaging in school visits to ILSs and frequently cite their lack of knowledge as a core reason. By beginning to understand the different identities that ILSs can have, and becoming more familiar with how they work through Bourdieu's conceptual framework, we not only become more confident in our own understanding and use of them but can develop children's life-long enjoyment of and engagement with them.

Although Bourdieu's concepts are particularly helpful in supporting our understanding of organisations with strong social structures, such as ILSs, they are less effective in considering the identity of settings such as natural and outdoor spaces. While considering the identity of a place in terms of who uses it, how and why, is still useful, it is of utmost importance to develop children's connection with the environment and thus promote their 'nature identity'.

Understanding nature identity

An abundance of research (Leopold and Davis 1966; Baker 2005; Moss 2012) documents the growing disconnection that people in many parts of the world have from nature. In 1966 Leopold and Davis recognised the concept of 'landlessness and the mounting loss of a collective awareness of and admiration for the land'. Richard Louv, in his book *Last Child in the Woods* (2010), described this disconnection and landlessness as Nature Deficit Disorder. He eloquently defines the term, and describes the changes in society and consequent impact that this had upon childhood, resulting in this loss of a personal and collective identity with the natural world.

> For a new generation, nature is more abstraction than reality. Increasingly, nature is something to watch, to consume, to wear – to ignore. A recent television ad depicts a four-wheel-drive SUV racing along a breathtakingly beautiful mountain stream – while in the backseat two children watch a movie on a flip-down video screen, oblivious to the landscape and water beyond the windows.
> (http://richardlouv.com/books/last-child/excerpt, accessed June 2014)

Louv identifies how, as a society, we are 'scaring children straight out of the woods and fields' and teaching them to avoid direct experience with nature. He argues that, subconsciously, schools, urban design, laws and cultural values all collaborate in delivering this message. While Louv reflects upon experiences within the United States, recent research in the UK reflects a mirror image of his arguments. Moss (2012) identifies how children in the UK now spend on average 17 hours a week watching TV (a 12 per cent rise since 2007) and 20 hours online. The RSPB (www.rspb.org.uk) highlights a 75 per cent decline in children playing out in natural spaces, while the UK government (2011) has reported that the likelihood of children visiting any green space has halved in a generation, with some groups having fewer opportunities to access nature than others, suggesting a widening social gap.

The evidence overwhelmingly concurs with Louv. Moss (2012) and the Council for Learning Outside the Classroom (CLOtC) suggest multiple reasons for this disconnection, including a growing obsession with zero-risk activities. All recognise the key role that primary schools have in 'turning this tide'. Consecutive governments (2005, 2010) and organisations recognise this issue and the pivotal role that primary schools can play in reconnecting children to nature and the outdoors. Through understanding nature identity, teachers and schools will be more able to achieve this goal.

The identity of a natural being

The RSPB report, 'Give Nature a Home', provides a clear message about needing to reconnect children to their nature identity. Human history illustrates the deep innate connection that we have had with the land and the natural environment. Our attitudes towards nature have been defined and changed by resource acquisition, but what appears to remain consistent is what Wilson (1993) suggests is an innate emotional affiliation to other living organisms, and a deep-seated need to be connected to nature for our physical and emotional health and well-being. Both Moss (2012) and Beames *et al.* (2012) provide a good introduction to this.

Reflection points

- *What opportunity do you give to children to learn outside?*
- *Do you recognise Nature Deficit Disorder in your classroom?*

The Learning Outside the Classroom curriculum

LOtC is not considered a curriculum subject and therefore does not have a defined framework within the English curriculum, unlike other curriculums. However it is implied and referred to within both the aims and individual subject frameworks of the curriculum. It is important to be aware of the curriculum aims as these can sometimes get overlooked and rather lost within the frameworks.

LOtC has an important role in meeting the curriculum aims of:

- promoting the spiritual, moral, cultural, mental and physical development of pupils at the school and of society
- preparing pupils at the school for the opportunities, responsibilities and experiences of later life.

LOtC is essential to effective learning within all the individual subject disciples and is embedded although sometimes implied rather than explicit within their frameworks. It is impossible for example to achieve the aims of the Art & Design curriculum without viewing the work of artists in our art galleries or using the environment as a source of inspiration, as artists do.

Equally the history curriculum cannot be met in any meaningful manner without learning about the past through museums, visits to historical sites or exploring the environment. Ofsted (2008) recognised this role, and how LOtC raises attainment within individual subjects, and has recommended that it be a feature of all curriculum areas. Research shows a myriad of benefits, which include stimulating motivation, developing an awareness of how we learn, supporting key skills, and developing responsible and active citizens (DfE 2006; Beames *et al.* 2012; Henley 2012; Moss 2012).

It is important to note that the National Curriculum forms just part of the curriculum that schools can provide for their pupils, and they are encouraged to assert some freedom and autonomy to include other subjects or topics in planning and designing a curriculum that supports their children and community. This provides opportunities for teachers to be creative, innovative and imaginative in their curriculum designs. LOtC is an essential ingredient in the achievement of this outcome. The DfE (2011) Teachers Standards explicitly recognise the importance of teachers being able to plan and teach LOtC effectively. They include:

- enjoyment of nature
- developing empathy for creatures
- creating a sense of oneness with nature
- developing a sense of responsibility.

Each of these aspects contributes to the overall development of a personal nature identity and can easily be embedded within the primary curriculum. Csikszentmihalyi (2008) emphasises the importance of enjoyment as a key to triggering intrinsic motivation and the state of 'flow' required for effective learning. Enjoyment of nature is inextricably linked to our understanding and engagement with it. We therefore need to understand the ways in which we can and do experience nature, and promote these four aspects.

Literature abounds with accounts of children playing in the natural environment and the joy and understanding acquired from it. Play is critical to enjoyment, and the way we engage with and learn about the world. It is part of our natural identity. Lester and Maudsley (2007) describe how experiences of playing with and in nature instils a sense of wonder, supports a sense of personal attachment to a place, and develops an individual's sense of self and recognition of their interdependence and interconnectedness with the natural world. Play provides a safe medium from which to explore familiar and unfamiliar situations and spaces. There are many different types of play (fantasy, creative, socio-dramatic, exploratory, recapitulative, physical mastery, object, etc.), which can all be deployed to support our interactions with the natural world (Hewes 2002).

Our nature identity is shaped and developed through the acquisition of various identities associated with nature. As teachers we need to be aware of the multiplicity of possibilities via which children can have contact with the natural environment, and how these can impact upon their nature identity. Children will experience nature through different positional identities (see Table 11.2).

Positional identities can support an understanding of how different identities engage with the natural environment. Children should be encouraged to discuss and to encounter these different identities in order to build a bigger picture of the natural environment, our interaction with it and how identities shape our understanding, beliefs and attitudes.

Baker (2005) points out that visiting the outdoors is not sufficient to build a connection to it, but rather is important in terms of how that experience relates us to the land. She advocates the use of 'Landfull' experiences (see the section on pedagogy, below). Landfull experiences recognise that people come to know places in different ways (think

Table 11.2 Positional identities

Learners learning from the natural environment	Poets, artists, musicians, etc.
Naturalists learning about nature	Field visits, geographers, botanists, ornithologists, etc.
Consumers	Using resources and products derived from nature, e.g. food, water, materials
Recreationalists	Walkers, climbers, riders, kayakers, etc.
Workers	Farmers, conservationists, gamekeepers, service industry, etc.

identities here), while challenging them to develop a consciousness of the land and their own relationship to it. It is through developing a conscious identity with the land that we feel a sense of belonging and therefore a oneness with it and all the living things that we share it with. This encourages empathy and respect for all living things, and a desire to care for and protect them, for it is when we feel that we belong that we care. Leopold and Davis (1966) observed how, 'We abuse land because we regard it as a commodity belonging to us. When we see land as a community to which we belong, we may begin to use it with love and respect.'

A nature identity promotes opportunity to participate in local and national debates that impact upon nature and our relationship with it. Alexander (2009) identified the need for learning to be real and relevant for children in the twenty-first century, and to empower them to be informed and active citizens. Louv (2010) comments on how schools make children aware of global issues (rightly) but ignore those at the local level. This is a missed opportunity with an array of issues (e.g. Give Nature a Home, Growing Schools, fracking, flooding) that can support developing children's nature identity.

Reflection points

- *Plan a visit to an ILS and reflect upon your own experiences of the space and how these have impacted upon your perceptions and attitudes.*
- *Think of three different positional nature identities that you have, e.g. a visitor, a conservationist, a child, a developer. Then consider what you would want to find out about the space, and research your questions.*

The pedagogy of Learning Outside the Classroom

...the quality of the interaction is of utmost importance. A poor experience during childhood could risk putting a child off future similar cultural activities into adulthood...

(Henley 2012: 12)

Partnership

There has been a plethora of research over the past decade alongside government reports and initiatives that have all identified the need for schools to work in greater partnership with ILSs (DCSF 2006; Ofsted 2008; Children, Schools and Families Committee 2010; Henley 2012). Research consistently highlights that, while the majority of teachers recognise the value of visits, they overwhelmingly report feeling ill equipped and unprepared to exploit the full opportunities they provide. Engagement by teachers on visits has largely been reported as being of a passive nature, with teachers adopting the role of 'policing' the class or 'sitting on the sidelines' (Griffin and Symington 1997; Mathewson-Mitchell 2007).

The issues are multifaceted but, according to Mathewson-Mitchell (2007), centre upon:

- minimum investment of effort
- insufficient tailoring to the curriculum and children's needs
- inability to integrate experience into the classroom
- ill-defined learning objectives
- lack of mutuality and dialogue between the teacher and the setting
- lack of self-recognition.

Bourdieu's (1991) theories once more help to explain some of the reasons behind the issues identified and how they can be overcome through working in partnership. Developing partnerships with the setting will support you in developing your own identity as an educationalist with the knowledge, understanding and skills to teach both inside and outside the walls of the school.

The three-part structure

Research evidence agrees that experience alone is insufficient for developing children's learning and that it is the quality of the encounter that matters (Baker 2005; Ofsted 2008; Henley 2012). It further identifies the requirement for teachers to use a three-part structure when planning LOtC experiences, involving:

1. a pre-visit stage
2. the visit
3. a post-visit stage.

The visit should not take place either at the beginning or the end of the topic. While using a 'hook', or stimulus, to capture children's interest at the beginning of a project should be encouraged, a visit beyond the school or local vicinity requires the process of orientation to properly prepare children and maximise the learning experience.

The pre-visit

The pre-visit stage begins prior to the commencement of the topic. Once the aims are established and the visit selected, you will need to arrange a pre-visit to the place. Growing evidence suggests that, although pre-visits are essential, many schools and teachers appear to book online and do not visit the setting or meet a member of the learning team until the actual day of the visit (Griffin and Symington 1997). It is therefore unsurprising to find that research evidence reports poor practice linked to a teacher's lack of confidence and knowledge, and that this is often correlated with no personal contact with the setting (Griffin and Symington 1997; Mathewson-Mitchell 2007). A pre-visit is essential and cannot be done virtually, in order to be both compliant with risk assessment procedures and to ensure an effective experience for the children. The checklist in Table 11.3 explains the rationale behind the pre-visit.

Table 11.3   The pre-visit checklist

A pre-visit is essential as it allows you to:

- analyse the suitability of the space and resources available for your children and learning intentions
- become familiar with the layout of the space
- personalise the risk assessment for your class and your visit
- collect photographs and resources to use for orientation
- tailor and personalise your visit to suit your class's needs
- refine your learning objectives so that you take full advantage of what opportunities might be available on-site
- plan your day, identify activities, locations and resources needed
- reflect upon what knowledge, skills, concepts, attitudes/behaviours the children will require for the visit
- discuss the visit with the learning team (if applicable to the site) and develop a partnership with them
- develop and extend your own identity with the setting
- develop your own 'illusio' (confidence and knowledge of the setting) so that the whole experience becomes pleasurable and will be more effective for you and your class
- book the visit; have a couple of possible dates for the visit

Resources to take on a pre-visit

Diary, camera, risk assessment form from the setting (often available online) and school risk assessment, lesson/curriculum plans, notebook

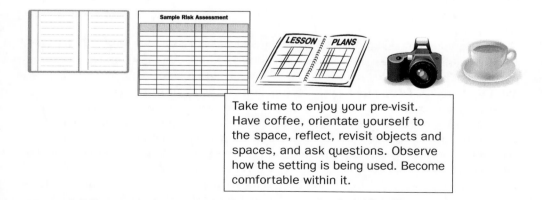

Take time to enjoy your pre-visit. Have coffee, orientate yourself to the space, reflect, revisit objects and spaces, and ask questions. Observe how the setting is being used. Become comfortable within it.

Bourdieu identifies how our 'habitus' (perceptions and dispositions towards new experiences and places) is informed by our upbringing and modified through educational and life opportunities. It is through positive exposure to new places and experiences that we begin to gain 'illusio' (a desire and belief that we can enter and play the 'game'). Illusio is acquired through gaining knowledge and skills necessary for that 'field' and the 'game', to enable us to feel comfortable and relaxed in the new setting. Developing partnerships with those working within the 'field' supports us in gaining the knowledge and skills required, and in developing an understanding of the mutual practices and aims that we share. Illusio takes time to build and requires repeated exposure. As teachers it is necessary that we acquire illusio not only to improve our own practice but so that we can also develop the children's illusion, ensuring that they become comfortable in new situations.

Hein (1999) identifies the need for learners to feel comfortable and orientated in a setting before learning can take place. Orientation is defined as a process containing four elements:

1. to feel comfortable
2. to feel safe and in control
3. to be able to navigate/find your way around
4. to understand how they work, i.e. museum, zoo, gallery, nature literacy.

The orientation process supports the development of illusio. Feeling comfortable in a setting can be acquired through previous experience, but should also come from the planning process. As teachers we need to remember that the children in our class will not necessarily have the same habitus and therefore their attitudes towards situations will be different. Orientation allows the teacher to build the children's understanding about the setting or place to be visited. It should be established where they will be going, why, what they will be doing and who they will be meeting. It is particularly effective to encourage the class to collectively write the risk assessment for the visit. You could provide them with a PowerPoint containing photographs of the setting, the spaces they will be working in, plan/maps of the setting, and maybe images of particular features/objects and people. This provides ownership, allows them to learn and manage their own risk, to understand the reasons for certain rules and to feel some control over the experience. While you will have completed your own risk assessment on your pre-visit, this will now enable you to facilitate by providing relevant questions and prompts so that the children cover all that is required.

In addition you need to identify what knowledge/concepts, skills and attitudes you feel the children will need in order to successfully negotiate the visit. These need to be planned and developed before the visit so that the children gain confidence and success during the visit. Csikszentmihalyi (1997) identified the need to correlate the balance between skill and challenge in order to maximise both learning and motivation. Ensuring children have some prior knowledge of and skills in the subject they are going to find out about will not only make them feel more confident within the setting but will also allow learning to be accelerated, and enable the expertise of the staff and resources from the setting to be fully utilised.

Within orientation lies the notion of developing the children's understanding of the 'literacy' of a place and learning about how the place works. What features does it have?

Who works/lives there? How you can learn and use the place? Children need to be introduced to and find out about a setting before visiting so that they can acquire the knowledge and skills they need to be able to effectively negotiate and learn within it. This could be done through stories, visitors, loan objects, role play and other activities. When visiting an ILS they need to be introduced to the concept of 'silent pedagogy' – the methods that the setting uses to support learners, e.g. information boards, captions, videos, interactive devices. In building their understanding of how to learn in the space, we are making them effective life-long learners.

The visit

In planning your visit always ensure that you begin it with an orientation activity. Children are entering an unfamiliar environment and one that is full of rich stimuli, sounds and smells. They require time to acclimatise and explore the space and feel comfortable in it before settling and focusing on the learning activities you have planned. Orientation activities should be short (no more than 20 minutes) and allow free choice and movement around the space, while providing some structure.

Research (Tunnicliffe 1995; Griffin and Symington 1997; Falk and Storksdieck 2000) identifies the importance of allowing children to learn in a personal, social and contextual way. They learn best in small groups with a 'more able other', imitating the family context, and allowing learning to be developed and modified upon. Opportunities should be built in to the visit to encourage interaction with staff and other visitors to extend this process. Encourage the children to initiate their own learning and develop their own lines of enquiry and questions that they wish to ask to investigate and explore using the resources of the setting.

In designing the activities, keep the focus on your aims for the visit, building children's literacy of the place, developing their identity with it and incorporating the principles of multisensory, experiential and discovery learning as you would in the classroom. You may choose to incorporate workshops and resources provided by the setting, but should analyse how well these will meet your aims and whether they may require adaptation; this can be discussed with the learning department and changes implemented to make them bespoke for your purpose. However, teachers are capable of designing and delivering their own sessions within the setting using their pedagogical knowledge, and the very best visits are likely to be a joint enterprise between teacher and setting.

Ofsted (2008) observed that a weakness of many LOtC visits is the insufficient definition of the aims of the visit and assessment of how the visit has impacted upon the children's learning. At the planning stage you should identify how you will measure pupil progress against the objectives of your visit. This could be in terms of the knowledge and skills gained, but also in terms of the attitudes and behaviours that have been developed.

Post-visit

Once the visit has taken place it is essential that the learning is brought back into the classroom and built upon through further investigations, or by developing creative ways to communicate, present and share what has been found out.

The above approaches will support you in planning and delivering high-quality visits to ILSs and natural spaces. However, Molly Baker's (2005) Landfull Framework is a methodology that is particularly useful for consideration when using natural spaces such as the school grounds, the locality and the countryside.

Risk assessment

Many urban myths surround risk assessment and LOtC. Risk assessment is a statutory requirement, but both Ofsted (2008) and the DfE are adamant that it should not to be employed as an excuse not to use LOtC experiences. The Health and Safety Executive (HSE) document, 'School Trips and Outdoor Learning Activities: Tackling the Health and Safety Myths' (2011), encourages a common-sense and proportionate approach to risk assessment on school visits. HSE advice at www.hse.gov.uk/services/education/school-trips.htm, alongside school and local education authority guidance, should be referred to when completing your risk assessment. The HSE guidance is clear and provides five steps to follow in completing the assessment:

1. identify possible hazards
2. identify who might be harmed, how and to what extent
3. evaluate and identify precautions to reduce both the hazard and the potential harm that could be caused
4. record your risk assessment and implement it carefully
5. review and update the policy each time (HSE, www.hse.gov.uk/pubns/indg163. pdf, accessed July 2014).

LOtC activities involving the school grounds, locality and day trips are covered by the school, with consent normally being given by the head teacher and LOtC coordinator. The CLOtC operates a Quality Badge scheme by which accredited providers have had their risk assessments assessed. However, most ILSs offer a generic risk assessment that can be used as a starting point, but that must be adapted for the purpose of your visit. Residential visits and visits involving more adventurous activities, such as outdoor

Figure 11.1 Person questioning

adventure holidays, will usually require approval at LEA level and should be carried out at an approved site. LEAs and the CLOtC have a list of approved and qualified centres.

Planning for adult support on visits

There is no statutory requirement stipulating pupil–adult ratios; this is left to the professional judgement of the teacher and the school. It will depend upon the age, circumstances of the children and nature of the activity. However, you will require additional support on the visit, usually via a teaching assistant (TA), with additional support being provided through parent helpers. Provide time prior to the visit to invite them in to school and share with them the plan for the visit. Your TA and parents will require orientation and you will need to provide them with a pack to support them on the visit. Your pack should include information about the setting, a plan of the place, a timetable and prompts to support them with the children, e.g. what do you want the children to be able to know or do on the visit, what to look at and what questions to ask.

The Learning Outside the Classroom teacher's toolkit

Pre-visit activities

- Visit the venue and undertake a risk assessment.
- Try out some of the activities that you might want the children to do.
- Observe how the space is used by the general public, to see what is and is not possible to do within the space.
- Take a child or group of children and undertake a pilot of what you want the whole class to do so that you can evaluate what will or will not work in the space.
- The children can research the venue before they visit.
- Discuss how you can work in partnership with the education officers at the venue (if there are any).

Visit activities

Orientation activities within the setting/space
Orientation activities should be short (no more than 30 minutes) and should allow free choice and movement around the space, while providing some structure. The aim is to allow children to acclimatise and feel comfortable in the space.

Making connections
Provide each child with a stimulus (postcard, picture, captions or newspaper/magazine page). Set the parameters of the area they are allowed to explore. Give them 5–10 minutes to explore the objects/artefacts/animals/paintings/feature, to find a connection with their stimulus. Put them in pairs or groups of four. Each individual presents their stimuli and chosen object, etc. The other members of the group have to say what they think the connection is before being told. This supports understanding about how the individual creates meaning.

Pointless

Ask the children to individually create a list in answer to a question, e.g. 'How many different jobs and hobbies can you find in the paintings?' The children then get in to groups of four and select the two answers on their combined lists that they think no other group will have found. If no other group has their answer then they score a point.

Call my bluff

Children, working in pairs, find an obscure object that interests them. They record what it actually is and then make up two definitions of their own. They have to make them plausible so that they might trick the other groups into believing their bluff.

Find the...

Ask the children to find which object they think is the rarest, most expensive, most important, etc. They have to explain their reasons to the group and a vote is taken. The group can then strengthen the rationale before presenting to the class. A class vote then takes place.

Make a trail

Children work in groups of four. They have to select four objects. This can either be what interests them or you could give them categories that they have to select from, e.g. flower, plant, leaf, insect. The children can then either draw a picture, write a caption/riddle or take a photograph of each object to make their trail. They then swap their trails for another group to follow.

Snap

Ask each child to select one object within a space that stands out or is special to them in some way, and take a photograph of it. They should then give this photograph to another child and ask them to see if they can find it within the space. This activity will make both children look more carefully at their local environment, and also reflect on why something strikes them as significant.

Developing identity

Settings and spaces are all custodians of collections and, to understand the purpose of most, children need to understand that they are conserving and protecting collections of things. Children naturally collect things – e.g. toys, comics, Moshi Monsters – so this is a good place to start.

My collection

Let children bring in a part of their collection to talk about to the other children.

Write a label

Give the children an object and ask them to write a label for it. This can be extended so that they write a label for a particular age or group, and reflect upon the vocabulary and understanding of the people in that group.

Radar map

This activity allows children to become sensitive to the environment around them. It requires them to listen attentively and record all the sounds they can hear in each direction, and to identify those that are near and far.

Make nature a home

Read the RSPB report, 'Give Nature a Home' (see 'Online sources' below), and show the children the national campaign advert. Investigate wildlife habitats and then ask the children to design and make suitable homes for the creatures to live in. These can be erected in the school grounds and in their gardens.

Outdoor journeys

Devised by Simon Beames (see http://outdoorjourneys.org.uk/, accessed July 2014), this is a clear and practical approach to using the outdoors based upon children undertaking a journey in their locality. It involves three steps:

1. raising questions and lines of enquiry developed from the journey
2. researching and finding out information to answer the questions
3. communicating findings to the other groups.

Post-visit activities

- Create a review.
- Write a blog.
- Create a montage of what you did.
- Create a loop game of factual knowledge based on the visit.

To gain subject-specific ideas for pre- and post-visit activities, take a look at the toolkit section for each of the foundation subjects covered within this book.

Baker's Landfull Framework

The Landfull Framework is a methodology originally designed for outdoor adventure programmes, but that can be adapted to offer a useful framework to support UK schools in developing their pupils' nature identity when using the outdoors. The framework consists of four integrated levels as described below.

1. Being deeply aware

This is concerned with focusing children on observing and identifying features of the particular environment in order to identify its uniqueness. It is aimed at making us aware of what is in the space. It encourages the identification, naming and classifying of the creatures/plants and features of the landscape, requiring children to recognise how it is similar to and different from their home environment.

2. Interpreting land history

Here the focus is on what this land was like in the past and interpreting how the place has changed over time. How and who would have lived there, and how would they have related to the place? It provides opportunities to develop lines of enquiry and questions that can be investigated, and supports environmental education, local history, archaeology, and creative and imaginary work.

3. Sensing place in the present
Next, the place is considered in the present. Who lives here? What do they do? How do they relate to the landscape? What impact do they have on it? What impact does the land have upon them? Baker describes sensing place as 'feeling a part of the story of the place', and says that this is how we assign value and develop a personal connection to that place.

4. Connecting to home
This is not only about making connections between where children may have visited and their home, but also making the experiences pertinent to them so that they become 'mindful' of them. It enables them to repeatedly reflect on and build on experiences, and relate them to their own everyday lives.

Summary of key points

- LOtC is a recognition that learning takes place everywhere and is not confined to a school building.
- LOtC can take place in four zones and involves using informal learning settings (ILSs) (museums, zoos and reserves, etc.), or outdoor spaces and places.
- LOtC supports the aims of the curriculum, and the effective teaching and learning of all the individual subjects.
- LOtC has multiple identities associated with who uses the space and how.
- LOtC supports reconnecting all children to nature and creating a 'nature identity'.
- Understanding Bourdieu's conceptual framework can support our understanding of ILSs and how to support the building of identities.
- The RSPB's Connecting to Nature and Baker's Landfull Framework offer approaches to developing a nature identity.
- A three-part structure involving pre-visits, the visit and post-visits should be used when planning LOtC experiences.
- Partnerships with ILSs and community/volunteer groups should be developed and embedded within the LOtC experience and planning process.
- Teachers should employ effective learning approaches using multisensory and experiential learning techniques. Visits should allow children to learn how to learn from, use and enjoy that space.
- Teachers should evaluate the impact that the visit has had upon the children's learning (knowledge, understanding, skills (subject-specific and social skills) attitudes, values and behaviours.
- LOtC is about developing the whole child, supporting their social and cultural capital, and enabling them to achieve well at school, and to become active and responsible citizens.

References

Alexander, R. (2009) *Children, Their World, Their Education: The Final Report and Recommendations of the Cambridge Primary Review.* London: Routledge.

Baker, M. (2005) Landfullness in adventure-based programming: promoting reconnection to the land. *Journal of Experiential Education,* 27, 3, pp. 267–276.

Beames, S., Higgins, P. and Nichol, R. (2012) *Learning Outside the Classroom: Theory and Guidelines for Practice.* London: Routledge.

Bourdieu, P. (1991) *Distinction: A Social Critique of the Judgement of Taste.* London: Routledge.

Chen-Hsuan Cheng, J. and Monroe, M. (2010) Connection to nature: children's affective attitude toward nature. *Environment and Behavior,* 44, 1, pp. 31–49.

Children, Schools and Families Committee (2010) *Sixth Report: Transforming Education Outside the Classroom.* Online at: www.publications.parliament.uk/pa/cm200910/cmselect/cmchilsch/418/41802.htm (accessed May 2014).

Csikszentmihalyi, M. (2008) Flow: the psychology of optimal experience. Harper Perennial Modern Classics. PhD thesis.

Department for Education (DfE) (2006) *The Learning Outside the Classroom Manifesto.* London: DfE.

Department for Education (DfE) (2010) *Transforming Education Outside the Classroom.* London: DfE.

Department for Education (DfE) (2011) *Teachers' Standards Guidance for School Leaders, School Staff and Governing Bodies.* London: DfE. Online at: www.gov.uk/government/uploads/system/uploads/attachment_data/file/301107/Teachers__Standards.pdf.

Department for Education (DfE) (2013) *The National Curriculum for England Framework Document.* London: DfE.

Department for Education and Science (DfES) (2003) *Excellence and Enjoyment: A Strategy for Primary Schools.* London: DfES.

Department for Education and Science (DfES) (2006) *Learning Outside the Classroom Manifesto.* Nottingham: DfES.

Falk, J. and Storksdieck, M. (2000) Using the contextual model of learning to understand visitor learning from a science centre exhibition. *Science Education,* 89, 5, pp. 744–778, September.

Griffin, J. and Symington, D. (1997) Moving from task orientated to learning orientated strategies on school excursions to museums. *Science Education,* 8, 6, pp. 763–779.

Health and Safety Executive (2011) *School Trips and Learning Outdoor Activities: Tackling the Health and Safety Myths.* Online at: www.hse.gov.uk/services/education/school-trips.pdf.

Hein, G.E. (1999) *Learning in Museums.* London: Routledge.

Henley, D. (2012) *Cultural Education in England: An Independent Review.* London: Department for Culture, Media and Sport.

Hewes, P.J. (2002) *Let The Children Play: Nature's Answer to Early Learning.* Early Childhood Learning Knowledge Centre. Online at: www.ccl-cca.ca/pdfs/ECLKC/lessons/Originalversion_LessonsinLearning.pdf (accessed July 2014).

Leopold, L.B. and Davis, K. (1966) *Water.* LIFE Science Library (reprinted 1981).

Lester, S. and Maudsley, M. (2007) *A Review of Children's Natural Play.* London: Play England.

Louv, R. (2010) *Last Child in the Woods: Saving Our Children from Nature-Deficit Disorder*. London: Atlantic Books.

Mathewson-Mitchell, D. (2007) A model for school based learning in informal settings. Paper presented at the Australian Association for Research in Education Conference, Freemantle, Australia. Online at: www.aare.edu.au/data/publications/2007/mat07094. pdf (accessed June 2014).

Moss, S. (2012) *Natural Childhood*. London: National Trust. Online at: www.nationaltrust. org.uk/document-1355766991839/ (accessed August 2014).

Ofsted (2008) *Learning Outside the Classroom: How Far Should You Go?* London: HMI. Online at: www.ofsted.gov.uk/resources/learning-outside-classroom (accessed May 2014).

Research Centre for Museums and Galleries (RCMG) (2004) *Inspiration, Identity, Learning: The Value of Museums. The Evaluation of the Impact of DCMS/DfES Strategic Commissioning 2003–2004: National/Regional Museum Education Partnerships*. Leicester: DCMS.

Stone, D. (1992) Elementary art specialists' utilization of the art museum. *Visual Arts Research*, 18, 1, pp. 72–81.

Tunnicliffe, S. (1995) Talking about animals: studies of young children visiting zoos, a museum and a farm. Unpublished PhD thesis. King's College London.

Wilson, E.O. (1993) Biophilia and the conservation ethic. In Kellert, S.R and Wilson, E.O. (eds) *The Biophilia Hypothesis*. Washington, DC: Island Press, pp. 31–41.

Online sources

Louv www.louv.com (accessed August 2014)

RSPB report: 'Give Nature a Home' http://homes.rspb.org.uk/?gclid=CO2au5asicICFSXHt AodATsAyw (accessed August 2014)

Further reading

Barnes, J. (2011) *Cross-Curricular Learning 3–14*, 2nd edn. London: Sage.

Bird, J. (2014) *Lessons in Teaching Computing in Primary Schools*. Exeter: Learning Matters.

Campbell, H. (2013) *Digital Religion: Understanding Religious Practice in New Media Worlds*, 1st edn. London and New York: Routledge.

Department for Education (DfE) (2010) *Transforming Education Outside the Classroom*. London: DfE.

DfE (2011) *Teachers' Standards Guidance for School Leaders, School Staff and Governing Bodies*. London: DfE.

DfE (2013) *Design & Technology Programmes of Study: Key Stages 1 and 2 National Curriculum in England*. London: DfE.

DfE (2013) *The National Curriculum for England Framework Document*. London: DfE.

DfES (2000) *Languages for All: Languages for Life. A Strategy for England*. Nottingham: DfES Publications. Online at: http://webarchive.nationalarchives.gov.uk/20130401151715/http://www.education.gov.uk/publications/eOrderingDownload/DfESLanguagesStrategy.pdf (accessed August 2014).

Drinkwater, N. (2008) *Games and Activities for Primary Modern Foreign Languages*. Harlow: Pearson Education.

Edwards, J. (2013) *Teaching Primary Art*. Harlow: Pearson.

Griggs, G. (2012) *An Introduction to Primary Physical Education*. London: Routledge.

Hathaway, N. (2013) Smoke and mirrors: art teacher as magician. *Art Education*, 66, 3, pp. 9–15.

Henley Review. Online at: www.gov.uk/government/publications/cultural-education-in-england (accessed August 2014).

Jones, J. and McLachlan, A. (2009) *Primary Languages in Practice*. Maidenhead: Open University Press.

Lavin, J. (2008) *Creative Approaches to Teaching Physical Education*. London: Routledge.

Lawrence, J. (2012) *Teaching Primary Physical Education*. London: Sage.

Lightbown, P.M. and Spada, N. (2013) *How Languages are Learned*. Oxford: Oxford University Press.

Martin, C. (2008) *Primary Languages: Effective Learning and Teaching*. Exeter: Learning Matters.

Ofsted (2009) *Drawing Together*. London: Ofsted.

Ofsted (2011) *Design & Technology Professional Development Materials for Primary School*. London: Ofsted.

Ofsted (2012) *Ofsted's Subject Professional Development Materials: Design & Technology. A Training Resource for Teachers of Design & Technology in Primary Schools*. London: Ofsted.

Roberts, P. (2006) *Nurturing Creativity in Young People: A Report to Government to Inform Future Policy*. London: DfES.

Saville-Troike, M. (2012) *Introducing Second Language Acquisition*. Cambridge: Cambridge University Press.

Sellar, W.C. and Yeatman, R.J. (1998) *1066 and All That*. York: Methuen.

SHP Schools History Project. Online at: http://www.schoolshistoryproject.org.uk/index.php.

Taylor, R. and Andrews, G. (2012) *The Arts in the Primary School*. London: Routledge.

Turvey, K. *et al.* (2014) *Primary Computing and ICT: Knowledge and Practice*. Exeter: Learning Matters.

Wallis, J. (2003) *The Tadpole's Promise*. Australia: Anderson Press.

Wineburg, S. (2001) *Historical Thinking and Other Unnatural Acts*. Philadelphia, PA: Temple University Press.

Journals

British Journal of Music
British Journal for Religious Education
Culture and Religion: An Interdisciplinary Journal
Education 3–13
Language Learning Journal
Languages Today (the magazine of the Association for Language Learning)
Pastoral Care in Education

Websites

www.afpe.org.uk
www.articlesoffaith.co.uk
www.all-languages.org.uk
www.babbel.com
www.bbc.co.uk/religionwww.languageguide.org
www.bbc.co.uk/learningzone/clips/
www.primarylanguages.org.uk
www.retoday.org.uk
www.reonline.org.uk

Social media (Twitter)

@SchoolDirect_EH
@PSHCEassociation
@stonewalluk
@TeacherToolkit
@Thinkuknowuk
@CEOPUK

@TheNFER
@naldic
@TeachersPetUK
@EHUActivexp
@OnReligionUK
@PabloPedantic
@ProjectRS
@RDispatches
@publicreligion
@onfaith
@JIRDialogue
@ethicsdaily
@garybunt
@godwired
@NATREupdate
@RE_Today
@reonline_tweets
@RECouncil
@ReThinkREnow

Index

Lesson Planning for Effective Learning

Martin Fautley and Jonathan Savage

ISBN: 978-0-335-24690-8
eBook: 978-0-335-24691-5
2014

Lesson planning is the essential component of every teacher's practice and the development of a teacher's skill is built explicitly on a rigorous approach to planning. This goes beyond just written plans and includes a process of mental preparation, anticipation, rehearsal and performance - all essential elements of the craft of teaching.

Key features include:

- Under standing of key ideas related to planning an effective lesson
- Discusses broader strategies such as differentiation, personalisation and assessment
- Explores teaching 'style' and your role in bringing lesson plans to life

www.openup.co.uk

DEVELOPING INTERACTIVE TEACHING AND LEARNING USING THE IWB

Sara Hennessy and Paul Warwick

9780335263165 (Paperback)
October 2013

eBook also available

Interactive Whiteboards (IWBs) are now found in over 70% of UK classrooms (Futuresource Consulting, 2010). Yet research suggests that, at least in the initial years of use by teachers, they are used primarily to support pre-existing approaches to teaching and learning, rather than developing these in tandem with advancing technological expertise. It is also clear from research into classroom practices that, despite the need to develop interactive approaches that promote learning – in particular by engaging pupils in dialogue - evidence of the use of such approaches in classrooms is rare.

Key features:

- Using the IWB in tandem with advancing technological expertise
- To develop interactive approaches that promote learning
- Provide teachers with the rationale, model and examples they need to develop interactive approaches

www.openup.co.uk

A Teacher's Guide to Classroom Research
5th Editiion

David Hopkins

ISBN: 978-0-335-26468-1 (Paperback)
eBook: 978-0-335-26469-8
2014

A Teacher's Guide to Classroom Research 5E tackles the big issues and questions of education research and offers a clear framework for doing classroom research. The updated fifth edition retains all the features that have made it so popular over the past thirty years - such as a rich range of insightful case studies demonstrating successful classroom research in practice.

Key features include:

- Interpreting and analyzing data
- Reporting classroom research
- Linking to teaching and learning

www.openup.co.uk

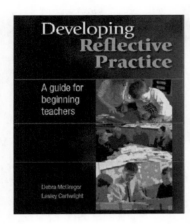

DEVELOPING REFLECTIVE PRACTICE
A Guide for Beginning Teachers
Edition

Deb McGregor and Lesley Cartwright

9780335242573 (Paperback)
9780335242597 (ebook)
2011

This student friendly practical guide helps you get to grips with reflective practice in teaching, through bite-sized sections that are informative and quickly digestible. The book clearly explains some of the best-known theories on reflective practice and then shows how reflection on and in practice can have a positive impact on classroom performance.

Key features:

- Case studies drawn from the reflective journals of beginning teachers in the primary, secondary and post-compulsory phases
- Short reflective tasks based on the authentic problems that beginning teachers face
- The inclusion of a number of new suggestions for developing reflective practice based on the authors' experience of training new teachers and supporting beginning teachers

www.openup.co.uk

OPEN UNIVERSITY PRESS
McGraw - Hill Education

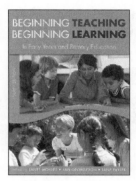

Beginning Teaching, Beginning Learning
In early years and primary education
4th Edition

Janet Moyles

ISBN: 978-0-335-24412-6 (Paperback)
eBook: 978-0-335-24413-3
2011

This book provides a range of practical ideas to support the beginning teacher and is written in a lively, thought-provoking way, with short, accessible chapters, cameos, useful recommendations for further study and end of chapter questions for reflection.

Key features include:

- Reflects the revised QTS Standards
- Provides more links to Early Years Professional Status
- Several new chapters on leadership issues, accountability, diversity and inclusion

www.openup.co.uk

Behaviour in Schools
Theory and practice for teachers
3rd Edition

Louise Porter

ISBN: 978-0-335-26272-4 (Paperback)
eBook: 978-0-335-26273-1
2014

Behaviour management in the classroom can be one of the most challenging aspects of teaching, but with the right approach it can be rewarding and enriching for both student and teacher. The new edition of this best selling textbook provides a systematic and thoroughly updated overview of the major theories and styles of discipline in schools.

Key features include:

- Outlines how teachers can develop a personal style in classroom management
- Explores proactive, authoritative approaches to discipline
- Explores aspects beyond the classroom

www.openup.co.uk

Teaching Shakespeare to Develop Children's Writing

Fred Sedgwick

ISBN: 978-0-335-26322-6 (Paperback)
eBook: 978-0-335-26323-3
2014

In this exciting and accessible book, Fred Sedgwick offers techniques for introducing some of the plays, starting with *A Midsummer Night's Dream*, to children between the ages of nine and twelve. These ideas will help them to write, act and draw in the grip of the greatest of writers.

Key features include:

- 87 lessons full of practical advice
- Explores Shakespeare's language: similes and oxymorons
- Various passages from Shakespeare's work

www.openup.co.uk

 **OPEN UNIVERSITY PRESS**
McGraw - Hill Education